I0750404

A Truly
Limitless Life

A Truly Limitless Life

20 Lessons About Motherhood and Life After My Son's Down Syndrome Diagnosis

Hidden Quill Press
LLC

Hidden Quill Press LLC

The events and conversations in this book have been set down to the best
of the author's ability, although some names and details have been changed to protect the privacy of individuals.

Cover Design by Mike Regina
Copy Editing by Enchanted Ink Publishing
Cover Photo by Elizabeth Canfield
Interior Photos by: Elizabeth Canfield and Mary Goewey

ISBN: 978-1-7376144-0-1 (print)
ISBN: 978-1-7376144-1-8 (ebook)

Library of Congress Control Number: 2021915434

First Edition

Hidden Quill Press, LLC
Oswego, New York. 13126

www.marygoewey.com

This book is for my wolf pups –
Nicholas and Marley.

Introduction

My son has *Down syndrome.*

I'd been saying this to myself in the mirror countless times. The first time I said it, my once long and curly hair was one big knot that would destroy any comb in its path. One engorged boob hung out of my untied maternity robe, even though I was sure I'd put it away already. I wore a heavily padded pair of disposable underwear left over from my hospital stay that caused me to waddle instead of walk. My eyes were bloodshot and swollen from all the intermittent crying. The bags below my eyes looked like two purple commas that hideously highlighted the major pause my life had just taken. The person in the reflection sickened me so much that I couldn't even make direct eye contact. Between the trauma and shame, I felt worse than I looked. My postpartum pain had yet to subside, and I was hurting in places I didn't know could be affected by childbirth. I didn't recognize myself on the inside or the outside. The only manageable thing to do was to focus on one task at a time, starting with this one.

A week or so later, I tried again.

My son *has* Down syndrome.

The eyes staring back at me this time looked like they belonged to a corpse. Nursing my son while failing to properly nourish myself made my complexion pasty and lifeless, but since I never left the house, my appearance was the least of my worries. Between my new, heavy chest and my lower back pain, I wasn't nearly as tall as I was before, which wasn't very tall to start with. How could I have transformed into this monster so fast? Just a short while ago, I was a glowing pregnant woman expecting her firstborn son and dripping in bliss. Although my pregnancy wasn't planned, it had gone smoothly overall, and I was feeling confident in what was to come. I went into labor while getting ready for the first day of my second year of teaching, dodging my fear of going into labor in front of my second-grade students. The thought of my water breaking during a math lesson had been plaguing my mind. Thinking back on it, that would have been a small stressor compared to what actually happened.

My *son* has Down syndrome.

I have a son? It didn't feel that way; at least, not the way I imagined it. I imagined this experience with a lot less crying and a lot more excitement. I felt robbed of the celebration I'd been looking forward to for so long. The reflection this time was still unrecognizable to me, but I was at least able to get my boobs to follow orders and stay inside my flimsy nursing bra. They'd never needed this much management before, but becoming a mother seemed to change everything about my physical and mental being. It seemed pointless at the time to focus much on what my life had been like *before*. Those days were gone forever, and so was the person I thought I'd been. My eyebrows were untamed, unplucked, and huddled around the bridge of my nose. I was furious at myself for having to practice something that probably came easily to other people. If I could react this way to a Down syndrome diagnosis, what other dark feelings was I capable of? Sadly, I would find out in the months ahead.

My son has Down syndrome.

How could this be *my* son? This wasn't the plan. Up until this point, I'd been the lead architect of my life, making sure to see every decision from all angles before acting. It felt like someone had thrown all of my carefully thought-out life plans into the fire, and everything I knew to be true about my life had turned to ash. I couldn't wrap my mind around both the diagnosis and my reaction to it and had no one in my life who could relate to my situation. I refused to let anyone in because I was judging myself enough without help from anyone else. I had no one to figure this out with but my husband and my reflection.

I needed to make a new truth, and I needed it to sound real to me before I set foot out of my house. I had to be able to tell people my new and confusing reality without the look of complete terror taking over my melasma-riddled face. If telling people my son had Down syndrome made me cry, I might get more of those unwanted condolences I was so sick of getting, but I was never good at holding back tears. I had to get better at saying this one sentence before getting thrown into the lion's den I imagined the outside world to be.

Eventually, after many practices, I stopped sounding like I was desperately trying to sell something that no one wanted to buy. The words were coming out with less confusion and more intention. I was making my new normal a reality with each humiliating practice. My voice had started to resemble the confidence it once had, and as I straightened myself to my previous height, I finally mastered it.

My son has Down syndrome.

There it was. It had been a little over two months since I'd given birth. I was asking a lot out of the floral leggings that were three sizes up from my usual, but that kind of stuff didn't bother me anymore. My long brown hair was clean, combed out, and up in a bun. I had some makeup on, but no mascara, just in case. I was starting to look like a human again. I could never resemble the person I'd been before, but I thought my family could at least pick me out in a lineup. As crazy as I was feeling, I wondered if they might have to at some point. I still had a long journey ahead of me, but I was on my way to healing.

> > >

I spent the first months of Nicholas's life locked into a schedule of nursing him every three hours and using the time in between to feel sorry for myself. The loneliness was debilitating, but I had no idea how to start the conversations that I needed to have, or even who to direct them to. Telling someone how I felt was an impossibility because *I* didn't even know how I felt. I went online and ordered all the books on Down syndrome the internet had to offer, and they all said the same thing: that having a child with Down syndrome is a blessing.

Of course, I know that now and can say with confidence that all of those books are exactly right. But in the beginning, it didn't feel like a blessing. It felt terrifying in that unique and unexpected way. I didn't feel ready, and I didn't want to change who I was.

Mostly, I was mourning the death of the *other* child.

The "typically developing" child I'd thought was in my womb was dead, and mourning him while simultaneously getting to know this new baby was a challenge I couldn't have prepared for. I desperately wanted someone to tell me the real deal about what they'd gone through *before* they found the blessing within the diagnosis. I wanted someone out there in the world to make me feel normal. Finding out that Down syndrome is a blessing is something you *earn*. It doesn't come to everyone right away. How could it when many of us were brought up to see it as a major flaw? If it came to you easily, that probably means you've already had the opportunity in your lifetime to know someone else with Down syndrome. I was not as lucky. The books I was reading weren't working for me because it didn't feel like they were written for the version of me that existed back then. They were written for mothers who'd already been living with this experience and had healed using their own resources, much like the version of me that exists now. Instead of finding the validation I craved, I found more fear and estrangement than I had ever felt in my life. Not seeing myself represented in those books added to the false belief that I didn't belong in my old world *or* my new one. So, since reading wasn't going to do the trick, it was back to scrolling social media to distract me from the self-loathing and pity instead.

One night, while awkwardly balancing my phone on the nursing pillow, I was scrolling Instagram in a desperate attempt to take my mind off of the uncomfortable way I had to sit to get my son to latch onto the nipple shield. I was looking at the search section, where pretty much everything that interests a person can be found based on his or her recent internet searches mixed with a good amount of spying. Thanks to that invasion of privacy, I happened to come across a family who had a child with Down syndrome. I almost didn't notice and scrolled right past them, as the child in question was not the focus of the photo. I slowly dragged my thumb back down to investigate the post further.

The picture was taken at a beach. There were three children. The child who abruptly interrupted my mindless scrolling used his arms to proudly present a sandcastle to the photographer. A child who was likely his brother based on his similar features had his arm around the boy's shoulders, waving with his other hand. A little girl, probably a sister, lay in front of their sandy creation having what looked like a true belly laugh. There was a group of hashtags at the bottom of the post, and among them was #downsyndrome. *Is this a real hashtag?* Even though I feared finding the same disappointment I'd found in the books I'd read, I clicked it. What I found within that link would change everything.

I didn't see a bunch of medical facts or unhelpful statistics. I didn't see a lot of unhappy people feeling sorry for themselves. I didn't see the one thing that I was absolutely terrified of seeing, which was people with Down syndrome being made fun of. What I *did* see were families. Young couples who had kids with Down syndrome. Women in trendy outfits and men covered in tattoos with their super cool, almond-eyed kids displaying their awesome skills for the whole world to see. Fathers and sons with matching hats. Mothers and daughters with matching bathing suits. They camped, fished, swam, and did just about every fun thing a kid can imagine. They weren't hiding their lives away because of Down syndrome but plastering them all over the internet.

They were proud. They were, dare I say it, happy. The normalcy of their posts was so refreshing. I finally saw people I could relate to. They looked like my husband and me and seemed to share our interests. Finally, I could see people out there who reminded me of myself and my husband, and they all had a child with Down syndrome.

After that life-changing feeding, I put Nicholas back in his bassinet and kept scrolling, despite wanting sleep more than I wanted oxygen. I spent the next hour looking at a variety of other hashtags about Down syndrome I'd discovered including #t21, #downsyndromeawareness, #theluckyfew, #nothingdownaboutit, and countless others. Those clicks led to more and more families. I found out that a lot of those beautifully photographed parents had blogs. *Jackpot!* Websites upon websites of women telling me similar stories to my own, raw and real, sharing even when it wasn't pretty.

As I read through them, I learned something I didn't know I needed to hear: I didn't have to lose my identity completely to take on this role. I could be myself, my husband could be himself, and we would find that Nicholas fits into our family—not the other way around.

> > >

Shortly before I began writing this book, a dear friend suggested I read the book *I Thought It Was Just Me (but it isn't)* by Brené Brown. This book completely changed the way I reflect on my time as a new mother. In the book, Dr. Brown describes shame as fearing that something considered wrong or unacceptable about you is going to disconnect you from other people or alienate you in some way. This immediately resonated with me, because I had an overwhelming feeling of being rejected from the world I had built after becoming a mom. Ultimately, I think I was afraid to be embarrassed. I was ashamed I hadn't been able to create the life I'd imagined—the life others expected of me.

Dr. Brown writes that sharing our stories openly and honestly helps us build what she calls *shame resilience*, which allows people to see our stories from our point of view, instead of judging them from the outside. Unfortunately, I did not find this book until after coming out of the depths of postpartum despair, but it changed my view of my experience, nonetheless. I'll use her ideas about shame throughout my story because this is largely a story about realizing that my feelings were not specific to just me.

I hope that after reading my story, other parents will feel the same.

> > >

A couple of months after discovering the online Down syndrome community, I decided to start my blog *Limitless Nicholas.* I planned on using it to help myself work through some of the feelings of shame I'd had around my reaction to the diagnosis. Now that other moms were validating my feelings, they didn't seem so isolating. I wanted to strengthen that sense of human connection even more. I figured it would be more of a therapy tool for me than anything else, because who would take time to read a blog about a sad mom's desperate attempt to figure out her life? I would soon find the blog to be much more than that.

The day I published the first post I was overcome with nausea. I couldn't believe I was sharing such personal things about myself with whoever came across the link. I was so private about his diagnosis before that, not even revealing the truth to people who asked about my new baby. Sharing the link on my social media would mean all of my friends and acquaintances would now know, and the thought of revealing my source of shame online was terrifying. I'd already been avoiding posting pictures of him on social media at all because I didn't want people judging him or saying he *looked* like he had Down syndrome. Back then, that felt like an insult. I thought I'd been protecting him. Now, I can clearly see it was the first of many times I'd held him back.

Before I knew it, the blog was being read *around the world*. Each week, a mother or father in a different country had discovered it. The connections I made with parents everywhere only fueled me to share more, learn more, and meet people I never would have met if I didn't put myself out there. I had gotten a taste of the validation drug, and I was addicted. Parent responses to my blog are what inspired me to finish this book.

> > >

Since you're about to enter the depths of our personal lives, you should probably know who we are. We are the Goeweys, pronounced gyou-eye. There's me, Mary, my husband Nick, and our kids Nicholas and Marley. Our family of four likes to have fun, and much like that family I saw presenting me with their life-changing sandcastle, we make family fun a priority.

My husband is a barber, and we met right before the start of my senior year in college at a pizza shop. Before I met Nick, I fancied myself an independent person. Somewhere deep in my subconscious was the idea that *my* goals and dreams had to come first, and finding my life partner had to come afterward. The plan was simple: career first, love second. I had the confidence down, but I hadn't even begun chasing a career yet. I definitely hadn't expected to meet the love of my life on the other side of a pizza counter, especially since I was the one working back there. I was just trying to pay rent and take advantage of free pizza and garlic knots while saving money on groceries.

I learned that love doesn't care what you had planned for yourself. Love just washes over you and not only points you in a new direction, but has you running toward it like you just found something you didn't realize you were missing. That was what falling in love with Nick was like, and I had the exact same experience when I fell in love with Nicholas and Marley. The love Nick and I feel for our kids has pointed us toward new paths that we never thought we could forge and has truly bonded us for life.

Nicholas, like his dad, is a party animal. Every morning after breakfast he walks into the living room and points to the smart speaker while making a little dancing motion with his hands. (Starting your morning with a dance party is a great idea, by the way. It isn't one of the official lessons I share in this book, but you should try it.) Nicholas has shown me that you can make a fun time out of the simplest things in life, such as squeezing a dance party in between breakfast and leaving for school. He has already changed the perceptions around Down syndrome for so many via our social media platform, and he has only been around for three years. He brings joy to everyone he meets and watching him have that effect on people has been the joy of my life.

Our daughter Marley is twenty months younger than Nicholas. She came into this world loud and wild, letting us know that her needs are just as special and important as her brother's. She bops around the house belly-first like a bouncer at a really lenient nightclub. Shoulders back, arms out, having a good time but ready to rumble at any minute. She is a perfect match for Nicholas, acting as a nice balance between teaching him to be considerate and gentle and not taking any of his crap. She taught him that not all toys in the house are for him, and although he didn't love the idea at first, he finally accepted Marley as co-manager of the playroom. Although our kids look a little like both of us in some ways, they mostly match each other. Their hair is sandy brown, pairing beautifully with their blue eyes, which is the opposite of their brown hair and brown-eyed parents. They are the source of our happiness and drive every aspect of our story.

The story I'm about to tell you is not about how cute and awesome our kids are currently, although I could surely write a book on that subject. This story is not always a pretty one and might even be uncomfortable to read at times. As Dr. Brown points out, people tend to avoid reading stories about shame. Of course, this book is not *only* a story about shame. It is also not *only* about the blessings I am experiencing. This is the story that I almost couldn't write but felt I needed to write.

I needed to create the resource that I couldn't find for myself when I was going through the diagnosis process: a story about someone like me who could not only validate my roller coaster of emotions but also tell me what I should do next. Since it often takes trauma for groups of people with shared experiences to come together, I want this book to act as a vehicle of camaraderie among parents of children with Down syndrome who may not have felt comfortable reaching out to those groups. I want to be there for other parents without them having to reach out and ask for my help, knowing from experience how hard that actually is. I want to be the friend that I wish I'd had when I was experiencing the initial diagnosis, the one who knew exactly what I was going through and could validate my feelings with the empathy I was craving. I want this book to spark connections between people who may not have connected otherwise. Lastly, I want to take the most valuable insights I've gained through this experience and share them so other parents can use the information to fast-track their way to the fun part of their Down syndrome journey.

There are a few things you need to know before you read any further. I am incredibly thankful that my son has Down syndrome. Not just happy—truly *thankful.* If a fairy godmother came down to change my son into a "typically developing" boy, I would kindly say "no, thank you," and wish for an awesome family vacation instead. You're going to read a lot of stories about initial feelings of disappointment and grief after Nicholas was born. If you're a parent of a child with Down syndrome, you probably understand this emotional tug-of-war. If not, hopefully, this book will help you understand a little better.

I also want it to be clear that I am not speaking for all parents. No two people with Down syndrome are alike, and neither are the people lucky enough to be their family members. I'm simply sharing the most valuable lessons I've gained through my experiences to help you cope, survive, and thrive after a Down syndrome diagnosis. This journey has brought me from my personal rock bottom to the happiest I have ever been, but that transformation did not happen quickly or passively. I had to jump over many hurdles along the way without having a chance to train for the challenge. If I could lower those hurdles for even one parent, this book will have been a worthwhile effort for me.

In this book, I share the twenty most important lessons I've learned about coping with the initial diagnosis and living in the world of parenting a child with Down syndrome. I broke up my bits of advice into three major sections: discovering my new identity, rejoining society, and doing the work. These were the three major milestones that I reached, and the lessons that I learned are based on the stories that happened in between. This experience with Nicholas has taught me an endless number of important lessons, but the twenty I chose to include were the twenty I wish I'd known beforehand and are followed by takeaways for new parents.

There'll be many times throughout this book where I compare my son's experiences or development to that of a "typically developing" child. With all of the research I've done around childhood development and the brain, I can tell you that children without a diagnosis of any kind have their wide developmental spectrum to fall upon as well. However, for the sake of consistency, I'll refer to children without a diagnosis of any kind as a "typical" child or "typically developing" child. When other people make these comparisons, they may have the urge to use the word "normal" to describe these children, but to me, that word is utterly meaningless. The only instance where the term "normal children" has meaning is in the *idea* of a "normal" child. Everyone has their own idea of what that means, but I'm willing to bet none of those ideas are alike. That idea can be a dangerous thing, allowing you to skew your perceptions of your own child. In truth, there is no such thing as a "normal" child, and the idea of there being this group of "normal" kids out there separates human beings in a way that, frankly, turns my stomach.

Speaking of words that turn my stomach, I still can't stand the word "disability." It's not an insult, but it feels like when that word is used, the focus turns to what my son *can't* do when what he *can* do is more relevant to his identity as a person. Down syndrome is labeled as a "developmental disability" or "cognitive disability," and I can see why that distinction is important when it comes to asking people for patience and understanding, but for some reason hearing the word when it's about my son is like taking a bullet. I want to put earmuffs on him every time because I don't want him to hear himself described that way, poisoning his mind with other people's limited expectations of him. He needs to believe he can be successful *because* of Down syndrome, not despite it.

If you're reading this as a fellow parent of a child with Down syndrome, I want you to know your child is just like every other child in so many ways. I think you'll find proof of that as you read since a lot of the lessons that I describe can be easily applied to typically developing children and their parents as well. Your child will be different in the most special ways, and I hope this book helps you gain this valuable perspective. The ways that make your child different from what you expected will take some planning and preparation, but it's nothing that's too impossible for you. I hope that while you read, you're comforted in knowing I'm right there with you in this experience, and that it's truly an honor to have a child with Down syndrome.

Discovering
My New
Identity

Who do I have to be now?

That's the thought that sparked an identity crisis that felt hopeless and never-ending. I had prepared to become a mom, but never a mom of a child with Down syndrome.

A strange stereotype existed in my mind about what a "special needs mom" looks like. I imagined her as, first of all, way older than me. I was only twenty-seven, and surely too young for such a burden. I imagined she didn't have much of a life outside of motherhood because her child's needs were too consuming, which meant that any aspirations she'd once had fell to the wayside. For some, this can be the truth, but in my mind, this was every single parent who had a child with a disability. Fear mixed with these grand generalizations had me picturing a life I wasn't ready for. I don't know where these perceptions of a special needs mom came from, but I'm willing to bet they've been perpetuated to me throughout my upbringing along with my misconceptions about Down syndrome.

So, was that who I had to be now? Was I about to let go of my passions and hobbies because my life was now on this new and scary trajectory? I'd never given as much thought to how I was going to have to present myself to the world as I did in those first months.

I eventually came to realize the same rule applies to me that will apply to my son someday. He won't have to change to fit a mold of what people think he *should* be. He can be whoever he wants to be in his unique way. I am a special needs mom now, and that only enhances me, just like Nicholas's extra chromosome enhances him. The journey to self-discovery was filled with confusion, but being his mom and advocate is the thing of which I'm most proud. It absolutely does *consume* me, but I love every second of being that person for him. My aspirations didn't fall to the wayside. Instead, they changed and are completely driven by passion. The stereotype that existed in my head couldn't have been more limiting.

Let me tell you what I've learned about special needs moms since then, both from becoming one and speaking to many. You see, we aren't like other moms. We've gone through things that other moms haven't even had to consider as possibilities for their children. We have to be sharp and more prepared, all while coming out from the other side of unexpected struggles stronger than before. We're brave because we've endured medical nightmares while staying strong for our kids. We're smart and research every available intervention we can to help our children succeed. We dare to put our pride aside to lean on other mothers for support, without worrying about appearances. We know the true meaning of needing a village to raise a child and build that village from the ground up. Some of the strongest women I know are mothers to children with special needs, and I don't think that's a coincidence. I feel blessed to be a part of this group, as should you. We've been picked to join the Olympic parenting team.

My favorite thing I've learned about special needs moms is that they'll be quick to open their arms and lives to you if you approach them, whether you know them or not. As I began the terrifying process of reaching out to different moms, I never felt that I didn't belong. I never felt that I was bothering anyone. I never felt like an outcast. I *always* felt like I'd found a new teammate on this journey. The only reason I hadn't found this right away is, simply, that I was too afraid to look. I imagine this might come from a place deep down within us where we want to treat others the way we hope society treats our children, so we make sure everyone who approaches us feels valued and welcomed. If you've been waiting to connect with other parents, consider giving it a try. I have yet to find one who isn't willing to listen to my story.

Once Nicholas's diagnosis was confirmed, I thought myself a bad person for being shocked and disappointed. I was the wolf in sheep's clothing who had no idea she was a wolf. Feeling such shame deep down can sometimes stop us from sharing our stories with others, but sharing our stories openly and honestly is a key component needed to stop these deep feelings of shame. Shame is such a smart villain; it blocks you from doing the one thing that can heal you, all while separating you from your natural allies.

As I opened up to others, people who didn't fully understand what I was going through were only able to offer me sympathy when what I needed was *empathy*. I had to gain a strong understanding of the difference between the two when I reflected on what it was I was looking for from my family and friends. Sympathy is simply feeling bad for someone experiencing something that isn't exactly relatable to you or just simply feeling bad for them for being sad. Empathy is something much more meaningful: it allows you to put yourself into the shoes of the person in pain by sharing their feelings and acknowledging that their pain is real and warranted. Once other moms validated the feelings I had of being disappointed in myself and my situation, I could finally move forward. They showed me *empathy*. They taught me that my pain was not specific to me and my situation. I didn't have to hide my shameful feelings anymore because they didn't make me an outcast. Their empathy gave me the freedom to change my perspective about the turn my life had taken. Those mothers knew exactly what I needed, and it wasn't condolences about a child who was alive and well. They knew listening and relating would get me out of my funk, and it worked.

When we try to put a name to the elements of our identity, we usually include the different groups that we belong to, such as race, religion, job, and hobbies. For example, I'm an American mother, wife, writer, teacher, and dog owner. Each one of those labels is derived from groups that have thousands of other members in them. I didn't feel like I belonged in a motherhood group when the diagnosis had just been dropped on us. I wasn't the mother of the typical child I expected to have, after all. I also felt like I couldn't join the "mothers of children with Down syndrome" group because I believed my reaction was so despicable they would never accept me. When I got brave enough to find that group, the other mothers showed me that I *do* belong. Confidently adding myself to that group allowed me to start building my identity back up again.

The truth became clear: I didn't have to change who I was for this. I'd still be myself, but a better, stronger, braver, more compassionate version than I could've ever imagined. I learned that my potential for personal growth is limitless.

The first series of lessons I'm sharing has to do with finding my own identity in this new role while allowing my son to find his without the burden of pre-existing stereotypes. This part of the journey was challenging for me, but I learned a lot about myself and my rock star son along the way. Before we could get to that point though, we had to travel the difficult road that was the mourning process, which was one I'd never traveled before.

Lesson 1

It's okay to mourn the *other* child.

It had only been hours since we'd heard the news, and I was still in shock. I kept replaying it in my head, trying to pull full sentences from the jumbled way my memory had stored the moment. *Down syndrome? Is she talking about someone else's baby?* While the nurse practitioner explained the situation to us, I was almost defensive with an aggressive confidence meant to stop a conversation in its tracks. My self-preservation instincts wanted to relay the message that nothing she could do or say could upset me. Of course, that wasn't at all true. I was hiding my reaction out of fear of being judged in my weakened state, but hiding my true feelings was going to take more work than usual. I was already feeling vulnerable in my adult diaper and flimsy bra and didn't want to add anything else to that list of uncomfortable traits. My hard exterior was getting more difficult to uphold with each passing hour, and I was starting to lose my grip. My blank staring was interrupted by a pair of nurses coming to retrieve newborn Nicholas so he could get treatments for jaundice. Watching them wheel my baby out in the clear hospital bassinet added to the deep feeling that a baby had been snatched from me.

Before closing the heavy door, one of Nicholas's kidnappers advised us to take a nap. I'm sure they knew how long we'd been awake, but we had no clue. The curtains did nothing to keep out the sun, which meant it must have been around midday. A "do not disturb" sign was affixed outside our door so that we could get some uninterrupted rest and successfully deter any visitors. I had no interest in having to put up a fake front for anyone else. I was happy to finally have some quiet time, but how could I possibly rest? Resting requires a certain level of mental relaxation, and my mind was spiraling into unknown territory.

As the sound of the rolling bassinet faded down the hallway, something came over me. We were alone and would be for at least an hour. There was no one to impress, no one to be embarrassed in front of. Just us. Me, and the person I was most comfortable with in the world.

The headache haunts my memory to this day. It was the most painful headache I've ever had, radiating through my eyeballs and down my neck. It felt like whoever was pulling my eyeballs in from the inside was also jumping up and down on the back of my skull. I lay there with my eyes closed because the light only intensified the pain. I remember being irritated that the pain medication I was on did nothing for my headache, as if complaining about that would allow me a chance to take some control back. The only thing more painful than my post-birth wounds were the thoughts running through my head. Nick lay on the blue fold-out hospital chair beside me. My back was to him.

As I lay there pretending to sleep, I felt uncertain about my soon-to-be husband for the first time in my life. *What's going through his mind? Is he mad? Sad? Is he mad at me for being sad? Does he think I did something wrong?* Someone who I'd always counted on and felt like I knew better than anyone else was suddenly a mystery to me. We are both believers in open communication, which is why our relationship has always worked well, but we never had the opportunity to prepare for *this*. The genetic blood test I had when I was pregnant came back inconclusive, so we assumed we had nothing to worry about.

The worries rattled around in my brain faster and faster. *Who was that child? What are we going to do? Will he need surgery? Will he be able to walk? Talk? Will he have a long life?* Pressure built in my chest. Usually, I have the mental and emotional endurance to suppress a breakdown, but I was too broken to stop myself. My true feelings finally had a chance to show, and I was too weak to conceal them.

I took a deep breath, and, on the exhale, I cried harder than I've ever cried before. I sobbed uncontrollably, hardly giving myself a chance to breathe. Within seconds, my thin hospital pillow was soaked with shameful saltwater. The crying intensified the pain of all of my physical wounds and exhausted me even more.

"My boy," I whispered between sobs. "No, no. My baby boy." Of all the words I had spinning in my mind, those were the only ones that could escape.

I wasn't calling out for my baby boy who'd just been rolled into the hospital nursery. I was crying out for my baby boy, who I never had the chance to meet. The boy I imagined having was gone, never to be seen again. The same boy who I'd read to so that he would know my voice when he was born. The boy who kicked my hands when I rested them on my stomach. I couldn't understand how Nicholas and "that boy" were the same person. They felt more like two different babies. The one I was expecting to come would never show up, and he was replaced by a baby I didn't recognize as mine.

I was only a few sobs into my breakdown when I heard the crinkle of the overused hospital chair behind me that probably housed hundreds of new dads before Nick. I wondered how many of those dads experienced this, and how many mothers experienced this while that chair sat painfully vacant. Nick got into the bed and wrapped his body around mine. For the months leading up to this, I felt like an enormous boulder waddling around to wreak havoc on any incoming doorway. I, of course, was still big, but the belly that had once been firm with life had turned to useless flub. Somehow, though, Nick wrapping his body around mine made me feel tiny. He was a protective cover around my shaking frame.

"It's okay, Mary," he whispered into my ear. "He's our boy. We got this. It's okay. He will have a great life. He is still our boy. We will be fine. He's our boy."

He wasn't mad, and I should've known it. I'm sure he felt that sense of shock and disappointment like I did, but his dedication to our family was stronger than that. This boy we made was our blood. He was a living testament to our love for each other. He was in our pack now, and we had to protect him. We had to be fierce. We had to work hard to make sure he had the best possible life. I felt Nick's determination in his embrace. He lay there and held me while I cried. Eventually, I fell asleep.

When I woke up, I walked to the bathroom and closed the door. I used the bathroom, changed my bandages, and as I approached the sink to wash my hands, I was startled by the creature staring back at me. I took a good look at myself and can still remember the horrifying image clearly to this day. The whites of my eyes were completely red from crying, reminding me of the "walkers" I've seen watching hours of *The Walking Dead*. The skin around my eyes was puffy and displayed some red pillow creases from my post-cry coma. The mascara I'd put on for the earlier pre-devastation visits was smudged under my eyes. My hair was in a big knot on my head, matted where the pillow had been. I wore a pink nightgown with a bloodstain on it. I didn't know how I'd gotten the stain and didn't care to investigate or even change my clothes, for that matter. That was my rock bottom. Just like I didn't know who that baby was, I didn't know who I was. I had also just realized what Nick had been looking at this whole time and wondered if I was scaring him even more than he probably already was. Moving on from this seemed impossible.

Our families showered us with food and gifts, all of which I felt I didn't deserve. Not only had I failed at my job of delivering the baby we expected, but I had the nerve to let the shock of this ruin our experience. I thought someone this upset about giving birth didn't deserve gifts. I wanted to be left alone with my shame. I wanted time to figure this out without the judging eyes of everyone around me.

Nicholas didn't open his eyes or move around much, which made it hard to connect with him. I so badly wanted that moment all other moms talked about where the child was born and immediately opened their eyes in recognition of their mother's voice. I *needed* him to look into my eyes to show me who he was so I could start to understand, but that took some time. Not opening his eyes was the first sign to the hospital staff that something wasn't going as expected. He was also struggling to nurse, which is something that creates a beautifully natural sense of bonding. I couldn't even feel reciprocation when I held his hand, since his low muscle tone didn't allow him to squeeze his fingers around mine. His hands felt so limp, and it scared me to think about what that meant. All I could do was hold him tightly and hope he reciprocated his love back to me in his mind, even if he couldn't show it.

> > >

The next time Nicholas needed his jaundice treatments was the middle of the night. As I watched Nick sleep in the wrinkled chair, I realized that even though I didn't know Nicholas very well, I missed him terribly. Since the late hour guaranteed no visitors in the hallway, I ventured out to see him in my nightgown and slippers. The dark and deserted halls reminded me of the post-apocalyptic shows Nick and I loved watching. No one was at the nurses station at the end of the hall. *Has this all been a dream? Am I waking up to the end of the world?*

As I approached a nurse came into view, and I was snapped back to reality. Surprised to see me, she let me back into the nurse's station where patients aren't usually allowed to be and gave me one of their computer chairs so that I could sit with Nicholas. He lay in an incubator under blue lights with a protective covering over his eyes that looked like sunglasses. Although he was just in a diaper, he seemed so comfortable and relaxed.

We got this, I repeated in my head. If any two people could handle this, it was Nick and me. I didn't know what it would look like, but I was comfortable with the team I was on.

I'm the type of person who makes jokes when I'm nervous. It's a weird tick I've had for as long as I remember. I think that deep down I believe if I can make people laugh at something, they won't notice the thing I'm hiding from them at the time, which is usually fear. I've always found myself laughing with the lab technicians every time I needed my blood drawn throughout my pregnancies. Humor has always been my security blanket. If I've ever felt backed into a corner in any way, I would lean on my wit to find something funny in a dark situation. Of course, with the way I was feeling, I couldn't imagine a time where I would be able to laugh again.

I started chit-chatting with the nurses to hide my nerves about what judgments they might've had about me. In my small town, the maternity ward isn't always bustling, and I was one of only two moms in recovery in the whole hospital wing. I started asking the nurses about their lives. We talked about things that didn't have anything to do with what I was going through. They asked about my life with Nick, allowing me to mindlessly tell them the story of how we met that I was so comfortable telling. Throughout the haze of fear and anxiety, I remember that as a small moment of clarity. Although they recognized our upcoming struggles, they focused more on the fact that I'd just had a baby, not a baby with Down syndrome. Sitting next to an incubator that housed my new baby, the mourning of my other baby dissipated, and I put Nicholas and myself in the same category.

This is my son. The same one I read to. The same one I've waited so long to meet.

In that nurse's station, I was able to talk as my old self to people who had no skin in the game, and that I would probably not see again for a very long time. It was comfortable, free of pressure, and helped me more than I could've guessed it would. They sat and listened to me, even though that's not exactly in their job description. They talked to me not as someone healing from a major traumatic event, but as someone they'd struck up a conversation with at their job. Our chat was free of pity or condolences, and such a welcomed distraction to me.

As I do more and more research around the topic of trauma, I'm finding out exactly how you're supposed to deal with people overcoming trauma: with empathy instead of sympathy. Connecting with people instead of making them feel like an outcast because of what they've gone through gives the person a sense of not feeling alone. The nurses probably knew exactly what they were doing, which makes me even more grateful for them as I reflect on those first days. They didn't make me feel like I was missing out on the "typical" baby who I'd thought I was going to have. Instead, they congratulated me and shared stories of their own children so that I could look forward to what was to come. Their allowing me a sense of normalcy in those late nights healed me much more than any medicine could have. If I could go back in time and visit myself in the hospital, I would make sure to tell myself these things:

The mourning you feel is okay.

It isn't a reflection of me, nor is it specific to me. I've spoken to so many fellow moms in my journey, and almost all of them felt this at some point after their diagnosis. Even though I'd had my baby, I still suffered the loss of the baby I'd expected. It doesn't mean I'm mad about the diagnosis, and it doesn't mean I should be mad at myself. I'm still me, and can still be the awesome parent I planned on being. There was once a time where I wasn't ready to celebrate Down syndrome, and that's okay.

Give yourself time to mourn the baby you thought you were having.

I couldn't even define the pain I felt for a very long time. It wasn't until I was able to recognize that pain as mourning that I was able to understand how to move forward. Taking this time without the input or overwhelm of other people was something I needed. Even though I had my new best friend in my arms, the loss that I suffered was real and needed to be addressed. It helped me come to terms with what was happening without people distracting me with how they thought I should feel. Their expectations of me didn't matter. What *did* matter was that I took the time alone to mourn so that I could heal, move on, and finally get to enjoy my baby. There is no shame in putting time and effort into mental health, and I've carried on this attitude since.

When Nick had climbed into the hospital bed with me earlier in the day, he said, "I don't care if he wants to live with us for the rest of his life. He can. He's our boy."

That was one of the first misconceptions that we were able to debunk through research. I've seen so many successful adults with Down syndrome who live and work independently from their parents. Researching the right way is the next lesson I learned on this journey because I did it wrong, and it caused me a lot of anxiety that I could've easily avoided. Lower anxiety might have gotten me out of my mourning period sooner, but I made the mistake of scouring the internet for false "facts" instead.

Lesson 2

It's okay to not know everything about Down syndrome.

Shortly after we received the initial shock, the doctor who'd delivered Nicholas came to visit us in our recovery room. He's one of those guys who has all of the kindness and compassion that should be required for this job, and we saw his visit as a welcome comfort. He acknowledged that we'd just received a huge shock and assured us that we would all be all right, knowing we probably didn't feel that way at all. After giving us some information about Nicholas's current health, he gave us some really valuable advice.

"Try to get some rest and stay off the internet."

How could we do that? During my entire pregnancy I turned to the internet anytime I had some weird pregnancy symptoms. I was dying to research Down syndrome so I could see for myself what I was getting into. I picked up my phone to immediately break his rule and realized very quickly it was filled with messages I couldn't bear to see. The screen was filled with "congratulations" text messages that I couldn't answer. People asked how I was, wanting my birth story and begging for pictures. Since my grieving made those impossible to read, I decided not to touch my phone at all. It would be days before I even charged it.

Before Nicholas came, I got my baby advice from lots of different places. My six years of experience babysitting my four beautiful cousins certainly helped a lot with the basic stuff. I was no stranger to changing diapers or applying diaper cream. My friend also had a two-year-old at the time, and she told me about all of her favorite baby products. Knowing that none of those past experiences could come close to mine shut the door on returning to those same people for advice on what to do next, and my unwillingness to talk locked that door.

Even though I attempted not to, I'm so glad my fear allowed me to take the doctor's advice. Once I'd come to terms with the truth and started to check out what the internet had to offer, it was filled with a lot of "facts" I've since found to be untrue. If I'd seen these websites in the hospital while I was so fragile, I would've become unhinged. When you originally read "facts" from seemingly trusted sources there is no way to tell that they aren't true, especially if your only experience with Down syndrome is with a newborn you've just met. All of the negative stereotypes and overgeneralizations I was reading made me fear for my child's future. I should've known better because I've never fully trusted the search results that would first appear on the search engine in the first place. I know that anyone can put any old thing on the internet, but when I had a baby, Google and I became very close.

Like all dependent relationships, it got a little toxic.

"Hey, Google, how many ounces of milk do babies with Down syndrome need? How often should they eat? What temperature should a baby's room be? I had the baby; why am I still so fat? What the hell is a sleep sack? Are my boobs *supposed* to be doing *that*?"

These were all nonstop acts of I-need-immediate-answers-to-feel-better desperation. Of course, when the results came up, they ranged anywhere from an online message board post from a disgruntled parent to a medical journal, and the legitimacy of the information was all over the map. Not to mention that I'd added the words "Down syndrome" to a lot of my searches when it was completely unnecessary. Basic needs are generally the same for all newborns, but since I was too obsessed with the fact that mine was "different," I figured those rules didn't apply.

As a society, we're a little too comfortable with the idea that the first results that pop up into our search engines are the truth. In reality, a source's level of legitimacy has nothing to do with their status within a search engine. Companies can buy their way to the top of the search results. When I started my blog, putting myself higher on the search results list was actually a paid option! It was an option I neither wanted nor could afford, but I was shocked to learn that anyone could pay to seem like a commanding presence on the internet. Sometimes, those results at the top are simply the ones clicked on the most, which doesn't necessarily mean they're accurate. Sadly, we're so used to thinking that because they're the first results, they're the right results. This way of thinking made it hard for me to wrap my mind around what was real and what wasn't.

> > >

The wait for the results of the genetic testing was mentally grueling. I didn't want to speak to anyone, go anywhere, or do anything. My radius extended as far as the backyard, and that was only when Nick forced me to get some sunshine. After we endured the shock, there was a long period of time when I didn't take pictures. I was disheveled, unrecognizable inside and out, and just not feeling like myself.

The last thing that I wanted to do was document it. Thankfully, Nick snapped pictures of Nicholas and me together without my consent on those days, lovingly filling the gap of missing pictures that existed in my photo memories.

I will forever be grateful for that.

I had to wait a long six days for the genetic results to be confirmed. Six days when you're up every three hours around the clock feels like an eternity. In those six days, I had a lot of time to imagine my life going in two different directions.

In the first scenario, I'd receive the phone call from our pediatrician saying it was just a false alarm. We would then for years share the story about when we thought our baby had Down syndrome for a whole week before we were told otherwise. Maybe we would express our "relief" in the results or our frustration with the scare. Either way, we would've gone about life never having a good reason to become more educated on this topic. All of that false information I had would still at this moment rattle around in the "truth" section of my brain.

In the second scenario, I imagined my life after the doctor called to tell us that the blood work confirmed Down syndrome. I tried to stay out of that mindset because at the time I still saw Down syndrome as a terrible diagnosis to receive. In this imaginary scenario, my life seemed bleak and unrecognizable. Since I didn't know what Down syndrome entailed, I couldn't even try to imagine it. I explained away all of his physical markers by saying that they just made him look more like his parents, and that was that. His eyes make him more like his dad. The gap between his big toe and the rest of his toes reminds me of my own feet, etc. Deep down, though, after spending twenty-four hours a day with him, I knew the truth. I just needed to hear it from the doctor.

I also had a lot of time in those six days to google things. I remember feeling so ashamed of myself when I finally googled this: "What do I do if my baby has Down syndrome?"

What do I *do*?

That was my desperation at its finest. I was all alone on Down Syndrome Island and didn't know how to signal for a rescue plane. I was mourning for some reason but couldn't put a name to why.

Even though my husband was the only person I felt comfortable talking to at all, I didn't want to unload on him. People mourn in different ways, and I didn't want to burden him further by adding "sympathy for wife" to his mental to-do list. Plus, he hid his stress to protect me. He'd seen what I went through in that delivery room, and he knew how fragile I was.

Six days later, the phone finally rang. We'd been impatiently anticipating this call, and I immediately answered and put it on speakerphone.

"We received the blood work back for Nicholas, and it looks like it is positive for Trisomy 21, or Down syndrome."

Even though I'd been expecting it, I couldn't stop the flood of tears that pooled in my bottom eyelids. I handed the phone to Nick so I could cry in private. Nick, as usual, took over for me in a weak moment and was surprisingly composed, probably because he'd been expecting it too.

"So, what do we do now?" he asked.

It sounded a little bit like my desperate Google search. I remember being grateful for the doctor's positive attitude. He listed all of the good things about Nicholas's health and development so far, explaining that his heart sounded strong, and he seemed to be hearing and seeing as well as could be expected of a newborn. He said we'd be keeping a closer eye on his health moving forward. After scheduling the next appointment, we hung up as different people than we were when we answered the phone. We sat in silence, but I knew we were thinking the same things. We were on a new mission. We needed to learn everything we could about this diagnosis.

> > >

If you're a subscriber to our blog, it might surprise you to know I wasn't outwardly telling people about the diagnosis right away. These days, my blog is filled with detailed posts where I dig deep into my emotions to be as honest as possible with moms and dads searching for someone to connect with. At the time though, I simply didn't know how to be open about it and didn't want to hear the responses from the people I told. I had some people telling me things like "oh yeah, my third cousin's neighbor's best friend's mom's sister has a baby with Down syndrome" in an attempt to be helpful. Nothing I heard seemed relatable, but even if it were, I wasn't comfortable talking about it to someone I wasn't extremely close with; not in person, at least. I couldn't keep my tears in if I tried. I also didn't want to be burdened with other people's reactions, since my reaction still weighed heavily on me.

Isolating memories like this was a big factor in my decision to write this book. I wanted people to be able to lean on me for support without being burdened by fear of judgment or trying to drive other people's reactions. I wanted more for other people than the results gave me the day I wrote that very embarrassing sentence into the Google search.

I had very little knowledge about Down syndrome before my son was born and envied those mothers who were able to deliver without fear. I knew people with Down syndrome were considered "disabled" and that there were some kids with Down syndrome in a self-contained classroom when I was in high school. In my school experience, I'd never been given the opportunity to interact with someone with Down syndrome. I just knew that "down" probably meant something bad, especially since I never shared a classroom with anyone who had Down syndrome. I didn't know why Down syndrome occurred, or how often. The only thing I knew for sure was that none of the knowledge I'd bring to the table in our new situation would be relevant.

Luckily, the school system has changed quite a bit since then, but the existence of misconceptions have decreased only slightly. Even general awareness is surprisingly low. I know this because since I began actively spreading awareness in my community, I constantly find myself telling other adults things they didn't already know and have yet to have a student in my class who already knew what Down syndrome was before second grade.

One of the first false facts I'd read was that Down syndrome occurs when older women have children. I was twenty-seven at the time and knew right then that I would have to look at these "facts" very carefully because I was nowhere near "old." Sometimes when I read statistics that didn't apply to us, my inner narcissism made me believe we were the one-in-a-million case that defied the statistics. However, I saw on social media that a lot of the moms were young like me. I got the idea that maybe some of the information the internet had to offer was simply outdated. I decided to forget everything I thought I knew and start from scratch.

Down syndrome has a wide range of physical traits that can come with it or not come with it. No two people with Down syndrome are alike. For that reason, comparing my son to the ideas being presented to me as facts about *all people* with Down syndrome wasn't helpful, since many of them didn't apply to my son.

Allow me to give you some general background information about Down syndrome so that you can start identifying and debunking the misconceptions that you may have.

What is Down syndrome?

You may be familiar with the common physical markers, but what is it exactly? Let's get down to science. Every cell in our bodies is outfitted with twenty-three pairs of chromosomes, one side from mom and the other from dad. You may have seen this chromosomal model looking like a ladder in school. I filed that chemistry class into the "things I'll never need in the real world" category of my memory along with logarithms and *The Odyssey*, so I needed a refresher. Two sets of twenty-three chromosomes are forty-six chromosomes in total.

If you have Down syndrome, there is a triplication of the twenty-first chromosome, giving you forty-seven total instead of forty-six. So, in every cell, there is a third copy of the twenty-first chromosome, which is also known as Trisomy 21. This only happens to about one in seven hundred babies, and its occurrence is completely random as far as doctors and scientists know. There is also an existing diagnosis called Mosaic Down syndrome where there is a third copy of the twenty-first chromosome, but not in every single cell. Down syndrome and Trisomy 21 are the same diagnoses, while Mosaic Down syndrome is a slight variation. You could have a triplication of many of the chromosomes, but Trisomy 21 is one of the lucky few that is not considered life-threatening.

This particular triplication causes a wide range of physical and developmental traits, but not every person with Down syndrome necessarily has all of them. The most common physical marker that most people are familiar with regardless of their background knowledge is the almond-shaped eyes. This is the one that tells people right away that they're looking at someone with Down syndrome. Some of the other possible traits exist beneath the surface, which we will touch on a bit later.

Now, let me explain it in a way that interests non-scientific people like me. This happens to also be the way I explain it to the second graders in my class each year. I call it The Lego Model.

If your body is a Lego model, your cells are the building blocks that help make the big picture. Your chromosomes are the little booklets you get with your Lego set that explain the step-by-step directions for how your body is to be put together. Maybe those instructions say that your Lego body will have brown hair or freckles. Maybe they will make you tall or short. Maybe the instructions direct that you'll be a spitting image of your dad. Whatever these instructions say will result in a unique model, which is why we're all so different from one another.

What happens when you get a Lego set with a lot of directions, and therefore a lot of pieces? The model is going to be a lot harder to put together and will probably take you more time to complete. There will certainly be more pieces to sort through and more intricate assembly patterns to follow. More directions mean more effort and more time.

People with Down syndrome have a whole extra chromosome added to every step of their "directions." This results in certain characteristics that can make it more difficult for people with Down syndrome to learn to do things, causing them to have to work a lot harder than their typical peers. For example, people with Down syndrome are born with low muscle tone or hypotonia. This is one of those common traits that exists below the surface. Because of their low muscle tone, it takes a lot more effort for people with Down syndrome to learn to walk, talk or master their fine motor skills. More directions. More effort. More time.

Will the Lego model get built eventually? Of course! It's just going to take more patience to complete, and maybe more skill from the people helping to assemble the model.

Why is it called Down syndrome?

Down syndrome is named after Dr. John Langdon Down, who is credited for discovering Down syndrome. By discovering, I mean he was the first one to make the connection between the physical and developmental markers of Down syndrome, and the chromosomal makeup that people with Down syndrome have in common. So, it's named after him now, the guy with the worst last name on the planet. "Down" syndrome? That *had* to be that guy's name?

Here are some synonyms for the word *down*: sad, melancholy, inoperative, malfunctioning, gloomy, and dejected. None of these were words I planned on using when describing my new baby. Do you see now why Down syndrome has such a bad reputation even when someone knows nothing about it? Why couldn't his name have been Dr. John Langdon Awesome?

"I want to let you know that your son is showing signs of Awesome syndrome. Here is some information. You will get the genetic results in a week."

"My son has Awesome syndrome. No, your kid can't catch it."

"Good news! Your ultrasound shows indicators of Awesome syndrome. Your life is about to take a very interesting turn."

If only those quotes were our reality. Instead, moms are often given this news along with some very confusing condolences. Some are even delivered the news directly before being encouraged to have an abortion. It seems crazy that it happens in this day and age, but many moms report to me that this is the case, and the pressure from doctors makes them strongly consider it. Luckily, we didn't have this experience. It wasn't presented to us as bad news; we just took it that way since it wasn't exactly presented as good news, either. To think that predicting a baby's value as a member of society just by looking at them seems a little unfair to me, but it's still happening all over the world.

Can there be severe cases of Down syndrome?

A big misconception about Down syndrome is that there are varying degrees of severity. When I was finally telling people about Nicholas, I heard a lot of things like this:

"I went to school with someone who had severe Down syndrome."

"My friend's cousin has Down syndrome, but it isn't that bad."

Sure, there are many health complications and developmental delays that can come from a Down syndrome diagnosis, and some of those complications are considered more severe than others. Some kids with Down syndrome suffer from congenital heart defects, which can be life-threatening. Others are non-verbal due to a mix of hypotonia and varying levels of communicative skills. However, not being able to understand someone or someone needing open-heart surgery does not make their Down syndrome more *severe.* It just means that they're differently abled than other people you may know with Down syndrome. Those of us who are considered "typically developing" have varying degrees of skill and health complications too. Some of us can run marathons with ease, and others would need a lot of practice and support to do so. Others can't even sign up for the marathon because there is a history of heart problems in their family.

Because of this idea, you must try not to compare your child with other people with Down syndrome or expect them to be like other people with Down syndrome. Would you expect your child to be exactly like someone else with their hair color? My child is one-of-a-kind, so holding him to standards that exist about Down syndrome would be a waste of time.

Where should I get my information?

There are a few great places to go on the internet to get quality unbiased information about Down syndrome. One of them is the National Down Syndrome Society (NDSS). They are the leading human rights activists for people with Down syndrome, and the information on their website is always accurate and up to date. I've included their information in the back of this book, along with a few other helpful resources.

Another good practice when researching is to change your mind set about what you're looking for. Instead of researching what people with Down syndrome *are*, try researching what people with Down syndrome *do*. There are some people with Down syndrome who are out in the world doing some amazing things. I've seen people with Down syndrome run businesses, train for triathlons, advocate for themselves in Washington, star in Emmy-award winning television shows, and even become international fashion models. I don't know about you, but I haven't done a single thing on that list. According to most people's standards, those people have outperformed me in life. It's a shame they were ever underestimated. Researching what people with Down syndrome have accomplished gave me a refreshed sense of hope and excitement for the future.

I would also highly recommend finding blogs about Down syndrome written by other parents. It felt like I had people with me for support when I was reading through those blogs. Their day-to-day lives looked a lot like mine, and there was a level of comfort that came with knowing I wasn't alone in the world. From a research standpoint, many parents blog about their child's medical challenges and overall successes, so you can get a taste of what other people's lives look like without thinking that yours will be the same. I've listed my favorites in the back of this book.

Interestingly, the first thing that tipped the nurses off that he might have Down syndrome is now my favorite thing about Nicholas. Nicholas didn't open his eyes much in the beginning, which made it hard for the hospital staff to examine him properly. When he finally did, they noticed white "brush marks" on his pupils which to them was a clear sign of Down syndrome. If you ever have the opportunity to see Nicholas's beautiful eyes, you'd see a deep blue color covered in white specks. His eyes look the same as the night sky, and I can stare at them all day. Something that was pointed out to me as a flaw is now my favorite thing to look at, and when I look into his eyes, I see every single star I've ever wished upon. Forget what you knew about Down syndrome and learn about it through your greatest resource: your beautiful child.

Lesson 3

It's okay to share the ugly parts of my story.

When we're not on parenting duty, my husband and I enjoy watching those reality shows where people are left alone in the woods to see how long they can survive on their own. One of those shows is a contest where the person who lasts the longest in the wilderness wins a life-changing amount of money. Some people are so skilled at wilderness survival they can stock themselves up on food and water and keep themselves warm with a nice fire all without a moment of discomfort. Because of that, they have all of this spare time to make a cool shelter with all the amenities they need while they wait to win the survival game. We're always so surprised when those contestants "tap out" early. Why would they give up on the money if they could easily win?

The answer is almost always the same: they miss their families.

No amount of prize money can encourage these people to stay away from their loved ones for another minute. Human beings are social creatures, and we aren't meant to survive in the wilderness alone. Being a part of a pack is what gets us through hard times, and our brains are simply wired to need other people. It's our instinct to crave connection with other humans. Through this tough period, I discovered the true value of connecting with other people with shared experiences, which is why human connection is a recurring theme throughout my story.

If shame is the fear of your flaws alienating you from the people you love, then sharing the sources of your shame can seem like an impossibility. I felt disconnected from the people in my life the moment I heard the diagnosis. I thought that since none of our friends had children with Down syndrome, they wouldn't be able to relate to our particular parenting struggles, causing us to grow apart from them. I assumed no one would understand, and I didn't even want to talk to anyone so that they could start to understand. I felt if I took the time to share with people what I was feeling they would silently judge me, and the pressure of that was too much. Fearing judgment from other people is a toxic trait I've since tried to become more aware of as I grow. It's fear that divides people, not sharing our stories.

Not only did I feel alienated from my friends and family, but I was also no longer able to relate to the one friend everyone has whether they like it or not: product marketing. This probably seems like a strange complaint since the common reaction to advertisements is general annoyance. However, I was alone most of the time, which meant I stared at my phone a lot more than I ever was before. This caused me to be subject to many more advertisements.

Strangely enough, having shut out most of the people I talked to regularly, I enjoyed those personalized emails I would receive every morning. It was correspondence I could count on, and one I didn't have to engage with if I didn't want to. After nine months of being pregnant and shopping for baby stuff, I was signed up for countless newsletters sent by baby product companies. To even shop or create a registry on many of their websites, you have to put your child's due date and gender so that they can offer you better product recommendations. Once the due date came and went, a lot of those companies would cater their monthly newsletters to my new baby's suspected age.

Some mornings, I would open my inbox to see if any of my computer-generated "friends" had contacted me and find an email that said something like this: "Good morning, Mary! Your baby is three months old today! He is holding up his head and checking out the world!"

Well, no, he wasn't. He wasn't developing at the same rate as typically developing babies. Some days, getting those emails was like taking a bullet. I could've woken up in a good place mentally that morning, only to be immediately reminded that my son's development was far behind everyone else's child who shared his birthday. This happened all the time, from countless baby companies. I felt so far out of touch with the world that I couldn't even relate to email advertisements meant for the masses. Their verbiage being specific to typically developing babies built the wall up around me even higher and validated the false idea that there was no place for us in the world. After already feeling like I didn't belong in my circle of friends, family, and colleagues, I wasn't even a suitable customer for companies whose mass emails were meant to reach as many buyers as possible. I didn't know where to go from there, so I dug my son and me deeper into our hole and hid, with only my phone and a few chosen social media platforms to keep us company.

> > >

Every year, part of the second-grade curriculum I'm responsible for teaching includes a unit about insects where we learn about the difference between social and solitary creatures. Some insects are social creatures, which means they need each other to survive, and others are solitary creatures, which means they don't rely on any other insects to survive. For example, a butterfly is a solitary creature. It starts as a caterpillar, then builds its chrysalis, and becomes a butterfly all without the help of any other butterflies. Bees, on the other hand, have hives where every bee has its task within the community that helps all the bees in the hive.

Human beings are social creatures, and I make sure my students hear this loud and clear. We are not built to endure our problems alone. We live and thrive in communities, and we need other people to get through the hardest times. When we don't have those people, we are hard-wired to feel the pain of missing them, like the contestants on the wilderness show always do. Why, then, is it so normal to hide our pain away from other humans in our community? Why are we so afraid to be vulnerable in front of other people?

My husband was an amazing support system for me, but I was still starving to talk to someone who'd gone through *exactly* what I did. He experienced the shock and original grief of the diagnosis, but not the same way that I had. My shock was coupled with severe physical pain and the ripping of Nicholas out of the womb. I loved reading the mom blogs, but there was still something missing. I craved the back-and-forth exchange of someone relating to me with all of the empathy and understanding I needed.

There was one blogger in particular I was a fan of. She had such a huge following on social media, and the reason for that was clear. She had a beautiful family made even more beautiful with professional-looking photography and quality content about real issues surrounding the Down syndrome community. One day, without expecting an answer, I boldly messaged her on social media simply thanking her for sharing her life so openly while explaining my current step in the journey. Just the act of writing my feelings down took a weight off my shoulders, and I closed the app thinking I would never hear back from her.

A few days later, I was shocked to see she'd answered me! She shared that she'd also gone through a grieving period, but that it was hard to look back on because her son was the love of her life now, and she wouldn't have him any other way. Knowing that even she, at one point, felt the same feelings I was so ashamed of feeling filled me with relief. It also made me realize that if it happened to the two of us, then there had to be more of us out there.

Lean on whoever you can.

As you figure out your new place in the world, make sure you're taking the time and making the necessary effort to find people to relate to. In many cases, you'll find the experiences that you thought isolated you are the ones the people will find the most relatable.

My husband was a support system permanently installed into my house ready to catch me at all times. Thinking that other mothers might be in this alone scares me to death. If you're reading this and feeling a serious lack of support, know that there's a wide network of mothers in your tribe that can be found online. We exist, and we're waiting to embrace you when you're ready. Even if you don't get an answer from someone, writing the truth about your feelings down somewhere can be therapeutic. It's like you're removing the difficult thoughts from your mind and putting them somewhere else for a while. I learned that my situation wasn't singular or unique, but extremely common. I would've never known that had I not sought out a community of other mothers.

Nurture the relationships with the people you decide to let in.

The mom-blogger I messaged also chatted with me about how important it is to nurture marriages through this tough time. For some reason, a lot of people felt the need to tell us about the looming statistic that parents of children with special needs are more likely to get a divorce. I'm not sure what drove people to say this to a married couple with a newborn child with Down syndrome, but it happened, nonetheless. I can see now, as I try hard to look at it from an outside perspective, how that could happen. Partnerships can easily fail when people are both not able to communicate their feelings in a real way or receive communication from their partners with empathy. If Nick and I both kept our shame surrounding the diagnosis and feelings of isolation bottled up, the tension could've become too much. That's why we value communication above all else in our marriage. If we can't come to terms with difficult things together as a unit, that negative energy is going to spill all over our children and stain our entire household. For that reason, confiding can't manifest itself as one-way unloading.

Maybe you're a single parent and your confidant is a close friend or relative. Those relationships still need to be actively nurtured through this time. There are a lot of added stressors that wouldn't exist with a typical child, like extra doctor's appointments, IEP meetings, and the revolving door of therapies. Balancing that with caring for your relationships is more difficult now, but also more important than ever. It could be easy to have Down syndrome topics be all you talk about, but you can't let that happen. If it does, your confidant might eventually feel like their feelings aren't being valued.

The communication and understanding that you crave goes both ways. Those people are around you because they feel safe in your company. It would be a shame to push people away when you are in a place of needing them the most. When I feel like I can't possibly take on anything else, least of all the burden of my friends' problems, I remember the nurses in the nursery when I was visiting

Nicholas in the middle of the night. Listening to the nurses tell me about their lives gave me nostalgia for the life I had before children came along and consumed it. So, think of it as not only being a quality friend to the people closest to you but also as nurturing your own sanity as well.

Be patient with your friends and family.

Something unexpected happened to me after I had each one of my children. After going through what we went through with Nicholas, I would see pictures of my pregnant self, or even pictures from before that, and sincerely not recognize myself. I would look at that person and think *wow, there is so much she doesn't know,* or *she still has so much to learn about life.* The same thing happened when I had Marley even without the trauma of an unexpected diagnosis. I would see pictures of Nicholas and me and think, *I can't believe there was ever a time that I didn't know my daughter* or *what on Earth did I do with all the free time I didn't know I had.*

I didn't want to reach out to anyone at first because I assumed that no one would understand me, and I wasn't interested in hearing what they had to say. I had to take a step back and realize that since I didn't even recognize myself, how could I expect my friends, family, or husband to recognize me as who I was when they met me? They were also going through this in their own way. As patient as you want them to be with you, make sure you are also patient with them.

The isolation that you're feeling isn't real.

It's an illusion created by the shame society makes you feel about the diagnosis, which is based entirely on misinformation. I learned we cannot truly heal from our pain if we don't have a community. If more people are open about their experiences, it could erase the fear surrounding the diagnosis, or at least the fear of talking about it. Without knowing it, reaching out to that first mom gave me certain power. I was able to own my feelings by having to type them in a concrete way to someone else and put myself in a place of vulnerability. That risk was rewarded with validation. From then on, I was addicted. The best part of the work that I do as an advocate to this day is connecting mothers and creating a community around parenting a child with Down syndrome. I know now that the original diagnosis is a small part of a big, beautiful picture.

I unsubscribed to all of the marketing emails sent to me by companies that made my child seem invisible, and currently subscribe to companies that promote and support inclusion. I stopped staying quiet about my son and started shouting his worth from the rooftops. I changed the way I interacted with other parents and talked about Nicholas with pride. All of this happened because I was able to find my community and use them as a vessel for healing. If you take nothing else from this story, take the idea that opening up to people will help you and your child move forward in the way that you both deserve.

Lesson 4

It's okay to ask for space.

After three hours of pushing in the delivery room, I was ready to give up. I was in a fishbowl struggling for my life, and the crowd around me seemed to be doing nothing to help. I had my husband on my left, our close friend and nurse Aunt Carol on my right, and our doctor in the endzone. I was contracting every sixty seconds, which is also when you're supposed to push as hard as you possibly can. I'd done some circuit training during my time as a fitness instructor but was nowhere near prepared for this level of exhaustion. This was the real deal.

I begged the doctor and nurses for a break and felt pretty pathetic about it. In response, they'd tell me that I couldn't take a break and that I needed to push harder. *Push harder?* That brilliant idea would be fine if I had one ounce of strength left in me. I didn't even have enough strength to hold my eyelids open in between contractions. I was so fed up with not getting a break that I boycotted one of my last contractions. Leaning back, I closed my eyes and pretended to be either dead or asleep. Both options seemed more desirable than the torture I was enduring. The other people in the room were quiet, and I could only hear the sound of *Storage Wars* playing on the TV in the background. Yes, reality stars were auctioning for storage units filled with deserted junk during my son's birth. While the auctioneer was rambling on, I remember thinking, *Maybe now they'll just put me out of my misery and save this baby.*

Since my pushes weren't cutting it our doctor had to make the difficult decision to perform an episiotomy and pull the baby out using a vacuum. I'm thankful he did, because I was losing faith in my abilities to do it myself with every failed push. The pushes were getting weaker instead of stronger, and I could feel my body giving up. To my own shock and horror, there was no time for the anesthesia to kick in, and feeling those cuts added to my trauma. That didn't matter, though. What mattered was that my baby was no longer trapped in the birth canal and was breathing air for the first time.

There's no way to properly describe the relief you feel after giving birth. It is like some chemical reaction is taking away all of the pain instantly and replacing it with love. In a split second, you go from being in the worst pain of your life to having relief wash over you like a silk tidal wave. There's a moment of transition, and any survival methods previously used for your benefit are now completely redirected toward protecting your baby. They put him on my chest, skin to skin, and covered us both with a blanket. It was as if I'd taken my chunky hospital remote and muted all the voices of the room. He and I were the only two people on Earth.

"Hi, Nicholas," I whispered.

As I started to register other people again, I noticed Nick tearing up in my peripheral vision. Upon arriving at the hospital, we were still torn between the names Nicholas and Benjamin and were waiting to see what he looked like to make a decision. I knew right away, because even with his eyes closed, he looked just like his daddy. Nick went over with the nurses and baby to the other side of the room to watch Nicholas get weighed and measured. He couldn't contain his excitement, which is one of the things I love most about him. Whether we're having a baby, or simply painting a room in our house a new color, excitement bursts from him like rays from the sun.

While he laughed and joked with the nurses, I "delivered" the placenta and got my wounds stitched up, all the while thinking, *How am I going to tell Nick that I am never having another child?* That was the most pain I had ever endured, and I knew for sure I'd never want to voluntarily endure it again. I thought people with more than one child must be masochists or just plain crazy. This was surely going to be our one and only child, and someday I would have to break it to my baby-loving husband. I figured that might be a problem for another more appropriate time, perhaps not while he looked happier than I'd ever seen him in my life.

Nicholas was returned to me having been wiped down a little and outfitted with a new hospital-edition "baby boy" hat and swaddle. He was born face-up, and his eyes were pretty bruised from scraping against my pelvic bone. He went from crying naked on the scale to being in a cozy blanket falling into a deep sleep. I remember not feeling whole until he was back in my arms, which is something I still feel to this day. I developed new muscle memory patterns for holding a newborn, which made my arms seem weaker than I thought they were. The shaking muscles in my left arm were the first indicators I would have to become strong to mother my sweet new miracle.

> > >

Trimline™

We weren't told right away that Nicholas was suspected to have Down syndrome. The bruising made it difficult for the nurses to notice the physical markers. We had a full thirty-six hours to live in newborn bliss before the bomb was dropped on us, and what a happy thirty-six hours it was. Our room was filled with flowers, balloons, and love. Every single thing about having Nicholas, whether it was a feeding or a diaper change, seemed so exciting since it was all brand new. We ordered Italian food from our favorite local restaurant, and it felt like we were on our first little vacation with our new family.

This was my first time giving birth, and I was pretty surprised by the aftermath. There were so many unexpected parts of me that hurt. The amount of bleeding scared me, and I vividly remember the trail of blood I left during my first trip to the bathroom. It looked like someone had just dragged a murder victim out of the room without bothering to clean up the mess. Although the nurses insisted it was completely normal, it felt really scary. Everyone that I'd ever visited in the hospital after giving birth seemed pretty calm and collected, so I tried to bury the fear surrounding my physical pain below the surface. *Nod and smile, Mary. Nod and smile.*

The flood of visitors started to pool in. Everyone who came needed their mandatory "meeting Nicholas" picture. You know the one—the visitor sits with the baby in the rocking chair staring down at them lovingly as if they are unaware of a photo being taken. I always asked them to send it to me because I wanted heavy documentation of Nicholas meeting everyone closest to us. My phone was filled with pictures of Nicholas at all angles. I'd bet all those pictures look the same to anyone else, but to me, each picture had its special majesty, none of which captures the true beauty of the miracle I created. There were times where I wanted to say, "Okay, that's enough, give him back to me now," but my politeness kept me quietly watching my baby get passed around. Little did I know at the time, my days of not doing what I wanted out of politeness would soon be over.

> > >

Around the thirty-six-hour mark, the nurse practitioner said that she had to speak to us and closed the door behind her. Instead of standing at the end of the bed, as all the other nurses had been doing during their visits, she sat down in a chair. I have to paraphrase this next part because it was honestly an irretrievable blur. I remember the main points of what she was saying, but to try and quote her verbatim would surely be as inaccurate as describing a house you'd driven by at eighty miles per hour. I remember it being dark, and the pink hue of the hospital room makes the memory seem more and more like a dream.

She began to explain some of the things she'd noticed while examining Nicholas as common physical markers of Down syndrome. She eased our minds that his heart and lungs sounded fine, but she recommended we get a blood test for Down syndrome. She was a little teary-eyed, not because she felt she was giving us bad news, but because she couldn't tell us a definitive answer. I'm thankful for her to this day because I know it must've been hard to deliver that news knowing it would change everything about our first baby experience. I remember looking between her and Nicholas as if to make sure he wasn't offended by what she was saying. Every time I heard her say the words "Down syndrome," I felt more and more like I was at the mercy of everyone else, and that things were going to keep happening to me without me having any say in the matter. I had the urge to complain as if a waiter had brought me something I hadn't ordered. How could she say this to me when I wasn't expecting it? This was not the baby I'd ordered.

After she left, Nick and I sat with that information for a minute. I went to the bathroom, and as I shut the door, a visitor walked in.

I didn't know who it was. All I knew was that I would rather die in that bathroom than emerge with anyone else in the room other than my husband. This was the first of many times in the coming months that Nick would have to cover for me in a social situation. I stayed in that bathroom as long as I needed to, and when I came out, I decided I didn't want any more visitors at all, and our once-bustling room became deserted for the rest of our stay.

At that point, the pictures stopped. There would be days before I picked up my phone to take a picture of him again after that. This gap in pictures will haunt my photo history forever. We went from having our hospital room be a revolving door of visitors photographing Nicholas as if he were on the red carpet, to asking the nurses not to let anyone past the front desk. The entire dynamic of our world had shifted. Once a social couple, we now turned the world away.

It's a strange feeling, being a brand-new mom. You carry this living thing around for nine months. You talk to it, read to it, and let others feel it kick. When it's born, suddenly it's vulnerable, out of its safe cocoon. It felt like someone removed a vital organ from my body, and everyone I knew wanted to examine it with their bare hands. I wanted to let them, but I also knew that if anything happened to that organ I would die. It felt like if anything happened to my baby I would surely die. After having two I still feel that way no matter how much time passes. Now that I knew my baby was more vulnerable than I'd imagined, there was no way I was letting anyone near him.

There are many things that we do that come from a place of social responsibility. Our society has dictated a lot about what is "acceptable behavior" and what is not. Perhaps you've gone to dinners you didn't want to attend but felt obligated to or gathered with people you don't necessarily like because it would say more about you if you didn't go than if you did. Maybe you've withheld saying something that you truly believed because you didn't want to seem like a disagreeable person. Whatever the case, doing something social that we don't want to do is a universal experience that connects us in one way or the other.

If you need time to process the shock, take it.

You don't owe your sanity to everyone because they're excited about your new baby. It's so wonderful to have people in your life who are happy for you, but that doesn't mean you have to appease them right away. If you need time, you should take care of yourself by asking for it. There were times when Nick was ready to show Nicholas off, but I wasn't ready to be social in any way. In those cases, he would have them over and tell them I was taking a nap. Of course, I was usually far too worried about my baby to nap. In reality, I sat in the dark scrolling my phone with my ears perked. I asked him to keep the visits short, and he always did. This way, I was able to allow Nick to have his social moments without having to be there front and center. I thought if one more person asked me how I felt I would combust. I needed people to stop asking me that. I needed to stop the new baby parade. Mostly, I needed to be able to tell people what I needed.

Tell people *exactly* what you need from them.

My in-laws were amazing when it came to making sure that I felt I was in charge of any situation. When we were still in the hospital, I could tell they were upset and going through their shock and mourning period. Of course, they were entitled to that, but whenever they came into the room, they never mentioned it. They did what they could to keep everything upbeat and made sure we were as well fed as we could be. On the first day back home, they decorated our house with baby decorations, filled our fridge with food, and told me something beneficial. They said, "You need to tell us exactly what you need us to do. If you want us here to help, we'll come. If you need us to leave so you can be alone, you need to tell us that too. Don't be shy about it."

This was so helpful because before Nicholas, I would never be direct enough to tell my in-laws I wanted them to leave. My mom had equipped me with better manners than that. I think they knew that about me and didn't want their presence to make me uncomfortable while I healed both mentally and physically. I also tried my best to nurse Nicholas, and it's stressful having people in the house during feeds. It isn't always easy to keep yourself covered up. Even if I could go to another room, I'd much rather be in the living room fully exposed and comfortable with my husband than alone in a rocking chair hiding from the people in the house. I was so grateful they allowed me to be honest. If no one has offered that to you, you should explain it to them and allow yourself the ability to tell people exactly what it is you need.

We had to use a nipple shield for the first six weeks before he could finally latch on his own. If you don't know what that is, it's like a little, soft plastic cowboy hat that suctions to your boob and essentially turns it into a bottle. To use this, I had to use both hands throughout the whole feed, making it hard to do much else. One time as I struggled with this, a close friend of mine dropped by unannounced to drop off food for the fridge and meet the baby. I was so frazzled and disheveled and didn't want anyone to see me like that. Add the stress of giving Nicholas a proper feed, and I was a wreck. I couldn't tell her it wasn't a good time because I was still a prisoner of my manners. I sat and visited, even though Nicholas was hungry, and my boobs were completely swollen. When she left, I broke down into yet another uncontrollable sob while I struggled to set up for the feed all over again. I could've completely avoided that if I were only honest and direct with people around me about what I needed. Instead, I allowed myself to be a victim over and over again.

Take control of your needs, and don't let others dictate what they are.

You're in the driver's seat and shouldn't let social etiquette take the wheel. If you need to send out a mass text to your family and friends asking for space, do that. If you need them to give you time to adjust to your new reality, do that. If you want to be surrounded by friends and family at this time, tell them that. Even if it feels uncomfortable to you at first, it is good practice for the advocating you may need to do for your child in the future.

Being honest with your loved ones and yourself about what you need will make you more comfortable, and you deserve to be as comfortable as possible while you are going through early motherhood. You're in charge. You had the baby, so you get to make the rules. You may need to speak up to protect your mental health during the postpartum time. That doesn't make you rude.

It makes you one fierce mom.

Lesson 5

It's okay to suffer from postpartum depression.

Unpopular opinion: maternity leave isn't as fun as it sounds.

I imagined myself floating around with my newborn and taking care of him while enjoying some time off. I pictured my days filled with trying out all our new baby accessories in between peaceful baby snuggles. I've had so many jobs in my life, often more than one at a time, and the thought of *only* taking care of a baby while at home sounded amazing. If you have kids, you're probably smirking at the page right now knowing I was a little off the mark in my maternity leave fantasy. Between the complete lack of sleep, overwhelming anxiety, physical pain from childbirth, basic needs not being met, and debilitating loneliness, it wasn't my favorite time in the world. All those issues aside, the main reason it was hard for me was that I suffered from postpartum depression.

Postpartum depression is an interesting beast. It's a deep pain, but not a pain those around you can see. It's more like an invisible monster in the room that lurks in the shadows and waits to suffocate you when you least expect it. You know the monster's in the room, but no one else does, and if you point it out it will attack. It's difficult to explain to other people unless they've experienced it. Even after you've exterminated this monster, the memory of it can haunt you for a long time.

People often confuse postpartum depression with "postpartum blues." The blues are something a little different but not at all surprising. As a new mom, you find yourself feeding a baby when you haven't had a proper meal in weeks. You change their diaper while having to use the bathroom so badly and painfully holding it. You listen to them drink so many ounces of milk while your throat seems to think you've crossed the Sahara. You lull them to sleep while barely keeping your own eyes open. You carefully bathe them even if you haven't had a real uninterrupted shower in ages. Gee, it's hard to imagine why we might get sad, right?

Postpartum depression goes deeper than that. When I had postpartum depression, I found myself in a state of sadness so excruciating that whatever used to bring me joy filled me with absolute disgust. The way I differentiate the blues from depression when I explain it to other people is that the blues can make you sad and irritable, whereas postpartum depression makes you think things like, *ya know, dying would be a lot easier than carrying all of this pain.*

I found myself thinking dark thoughts that I never had before. I thought about how easy it would be for me to just die and wondered about how my family's life would go on without me. When everything seems so hard, death sounds easy, like it did in the delivery room. I could simply go to sleep one day and never wake up, and then I wouldn't have to worry about this pain anymore.

Other days, I would think, *you know what, I don't want to die, but a nice serious accident causing me to become hospitalized for a few days would be a nice break from this day-to-day grind. I would also be able to get some deep, drug-induced sleep, and my meals would be brought to me.* It's painful to reminisce about wishing harm on myself to get a break from the sadness, but it's one of the things I have found in common with many of the mothers I've connected with.

If only this topic was talked about more with new mothers. Not in a way that warns us against it, but in a way that prepares us for it. There's so much shame surrounding mental health issues, and when people endure them, they're usually enduring them *alone* for that reason. I didn't dare tell anyone the thoughts I had. The only way that doctors can flag you as someone who's suffering from this is if you check the little box on your appointment intake forms, or if you outright tell them. Telling them isn't easy, especially if you hide behind your pride as I used to. It feels like asking for help is admitting to being crazy and risking yourself in some way. I told my doctors that I was extremely depressed, but never told them about the dark thoughts I was having. I didn't know what the protocol would be if I did and was scared of being separated from my baby. It's easy to label a woman as crazy in this country, and I didn't want to embarrass my son like that.

I went through postpartum depression with both my kids, which taught me that it wasn't specific to receiving a Down syndrome diagnosis. It can happen to all of us, no matter the trauma we may suffer in the hospital. This is almost as common as childbirth, but not talked about nearly as much. I knew ahead of time that childbirth hurt because it doesn't exactly look fun in movies, but I've never seen a character on a show or in a movie with postpartum depression. It is completely normal, but in no way normalized. I wish I'd known how common it was because if I had, I wouldn't have been so ashamed. Celebrities are always praised as courageous when they share their struggles with postpartum depression. Wouldn't it be nice if we didn't have to be courageous, and we were easily able to talk openly about our experiences even if they aren't pretty?

In the United States, it's pretty standard to return to work after six weeks. Sometimes postpartum depression doesn't even kick in until then. So now you're leaving your new baby for the first time *and* your mind is in an uncontrollable downward spiral, all while putting your baby's needs before your own at every given opportunity. Add job responsibilities, and that sounds like a recipe for failure. We aren't given a fair chance against postpartum depression when you consider everything stacked against us.

There's also a lot of pressure from society that comes with being a mom in general. Everyone wants to be *that* mom who bounces right back after birth and makes the whole thing look effortless. Our culture favors women who can pull this off, leaving the rest of us to feel inadequate in our elastic-waist jeans and jumbo bras. Sometimes that pressure can be too much and cause mothers to shut themselves away from finding healing communities. I'd done that and had to find other means of balancing my mind so I could be the best person possible for my son. This was the point in my life where I discovered self-care.

Self-care should be treated as a routine, not a reward.

Before having kids, I would've told you self-care is a waste of precious time and does nothing to get you to your goals. I used to treat it as a reward if I had accomplished some big task or survived an impossible week. I've since learned it's more helpful as something wrapped into your daily routines. Simple things like making sure I drank enough water and got a little sunshine every day would make me more clear-headed and positive, which would then make me more productive. I learned that if I put the time into self-care, I would get more time out of the day. Otherwise, my grogginess and crankiness held me back. So, when you're already battling depression, self-care needs to be the life preserver you throw yourself when you aren't able to get help anywhere else.

When I had my daughter, I was a little bit more prepared for the reality of childbirth. I wanted to treat myself as well as I treated my new baby and knew my sanity was riding on it. When setting up her nursery I thought, *What can I do differently this time?* All those miserable and lonely nights struggling to nurse came flooding back to me. Instead of only thinking about what Marley's needs would be in her nursery, I thought about mine. Nick couldn't get up in the night with me anymore because someone had to get some rest to take care of Nicholas. That also meant he couldn't help me when I needed things during feedings. The days of him spooning food into my mouth while I used both hands to nurse a delicate newborn were long gone. I was going to be on my own for those late-night feeds for the first time.

My husband mounted a TV so I'd have something to do in the middle of the night instead of staring at the wall as I'd done with Nicholas. I set up a nightstand with an extra shelf for my breast pump. I even stocked the side of the rocking chair with bottles of water and snacks. There was no reason for me to sit there starving and thirsty unable to help myself. The more of my own needs I was able to address, the easier it was to address Marley's needs. When she finally came, I was better able to wrap my mind around what I had to do to keep my head above water. I could still feel the monster in the room but found comfort in knowing that it would leave eventually. This wasn't my forever roommate. It would leave, and I'd be back in charge.

Whether you receive an unexpected diagnosis during your pregnancy or not, make sure to set up the nursery with your own needs in mind. Your baby will need a lot of support, but so will you, and it's important to recognize that as soon as possible. Treat yourself as someone who just experienced birth, which can be traumatic, not as someone who's supposed to have everything under control. You matter too, and you can't be your best self for your baby if you aren't meeting your body's basic needs.

Taking care of yourself doesn't make you a bad mom.
I used to be stuck in the mindset that if I took some time to take care of myself then I must be a bad mom because I wasn't using my precious time to focus on my kids. In reality, it makes me a better mom. By bettering myself, I'm making a better person for my children to grow up with. So, on days where I ask my in-laws to watch my children overnight, having no real plans that make it impossible for me to have them at home, I don't feel a hint of mom-guilt. I know that even though I'm doing something for myself, I'm also doing something for my kids. Even if my whole plan is to be at home preparing for the daily mom grind by vacuuming and grocery shopping, it's just a little easier to do by myself. This way, my kids can come home after their sleepover to a mom who enjoys every moment she's with them instead of a bitter mom secretly aching for a break and counting the minutes until naptime.

In high school, I had a health teacher who once said, "You'd never pour sugar into your car's gas tank, but people pour it and other terrible things into their bodies like they're of much lesser value. Why would you treat your car better than your own body?" This quote really stuck with me because, at the time, I had just acquired my first car and was doing my best to take excellent care of it while using it to get myself sugary, caffeinated drinks at Dunkin' Donuts. Of course, when you're young you feel invincible, as I did until the moment of Nicholas's diagnosis.

Your body isn't even capable of reaching its full potential if it isn't provided with enough water and nutrients to be able to work at its full capacity. I stopped only cooking nutrient-dense meals for my kids while ignoring my own nutritional needs. Catering to my own health better equipped me to combat postpartum depression. I finally had the tools to actively fight depression instead of passively waiting for it to go away.

Self-care isn't only about me staying sane as a working mom. It's also about setting a good example for my children. My children are going to grow up seeing me work hard to make the best version of myself so that they can have the best mom possible. I want them to see me eating well and exercising and know how it helps my mental clarity so that maybe they'll want to do the same. To see how someone schedules their self-care into an already insane routine because it's *that* important can send a big message to a child, especially since kids follow your example, not your advice. I want them to know that they should value themselves as much as they value anyone else and that there's no shame in working on building that value every day.

Postpartum depression ends.

When it feels like a never-ending spiral, remind yourself of that fact. Even if you don't turn to self-care and wait out the clock you'll come back eventually. You'll have evicted the monster and be able to find joy once again. You might find you have a different perspective on certain things after the experience. It's sort of like taking a trip to hell, seeing what it's like down there, and coming back knowing some things that other people will never understand. Now you know what hell is like, so events that would've seemed like a crisis before having children don't elicit the same amount of panic from you as they may have before.

When the depression ends, the memory of it polishes the mental clarity you work on every day with continued self-care. Once the fog is gone, you'll see your baby clearer than ever. Then, you can focus on the fun part: getting to know your baby.

Lesson 6

There's no baby like my baby.

If we're talking about finding identity, we can't forget about my baby's identity. If Nicholas wasn't the baby that I'd imagined having, then who was he?

For the first seven days of Nicholas's life, Nick was able to be home with me. We spent our first two nights as parents camped out in the living room with the bassinet in the middle of our couch and loveseat. We both got up for every single feeding, fueled by a mixture of excitement and fear. After we were done with each one, we'd reapply Nicholas's swaddle and let the cast of *The Office* lull us back to sleep. This happened every three hours without fail. Watching my exhausted husband in the blue glow of the TV making himself comfortable on the smaller couch, nobly letting me have the bigger one, I'd think, *How the hell am I going to do this by myself?* The night before his first day back to work, we decided I'd do all of the night shifts alone so Nick could rest up for his return. It was my opportunity to practice for solo motherhood.

When my alarm went off for the three a.m. feed, I felt the weight of the exhaustion more than usual. The bed was so warm, and the world outside was so cold. Feeling too tired and too depressed to move, I considered skipping it. If he were *truly* hungry, he'd cry, right? I was always waking him up, and not the other way around. Could I let him sleep just this once?

He was six days old, and still a complete stranger. His diagnosis represented a challenge to me when it came to feedings, as if someone bet me he would be underweight and I had to work hard to prove them wrong. The routine of it felt like a hamster wheel. Alarm, diaper, nurse, bed, repeat. As much as I wanted to hit "stop" instead of "snooze," I lifted my body out of the bed, took Nicholas from his bassinet and brought him to his mountain-themed bedroom. Even after gently placing him on his buffalo plaid changing table, he was still fast asleep. *See, he doesn't want to be up, either,* I thought bitterly as I grabbed the Velcro on his sleep sack. I slowly ripped them apart and watched his arms stretch over his head as I changed his diaper. The cool air entering his jammies woke him up, and at the very end of his stretch, he looked me right in the eye and smiled a big, gummy smile.

"Well, hello there!" I said happily, as if becoming acquainted for the first time. I was flattered that he smiled at me, not only because it was adorable and never-before-seen, but also because it felt like he was truly happy to see me and not just ready for the milkmaid to do her job. The robotic routine of motherhood melted away into excitement that my baby acknowledged me. I finally got that moment I'd wanted so badly in the hospital, where he recognized *me* as his mom. That night, he stopped being my newborn baby and became my little buddy. After slipping his skinny limbs into a fresh pair of jammies, we took our usual seat in the rocker with a new attitude. I wasn't flustered that it was going to be tough to get him to feed. I was excited that we were getting another chance to practice. That was the first of many times Nicholas was able to get me out of a funk.

In the process of getting to know Nicholas, I learned there's little value in thinking of him as "a baby with Down syndrome." I had to change my mindset and think of him as *my* baby. Since my hours of research had taught me there's no point in comparing him to other babies with Down syndrome, it seemed a waste of time to think of him that way at all. This one was uniquely mine, and there's no other baby like him

Getting to know my children and experiencing life with them caused me to redefine many things, including the term "special needs". Before Nicholas was born, when I heard "special needs," what I actually heard was "difficult." That child has *special needs*, which means it's going to be *difficult* for them to do what everyone else does. I didn't come to those conclusions on my own. I had a lot of help from the structures that society has put in place for people with special needs.

Sure, special circumstances might cause difficulty in certain aspects of Nicholas's life, like learning how to walk and talk. But Nicholas was such a great baby. He did whatever we did and adapted to most atmospheres we brought him to. That, of course, has changed a bit since he's become a wild toddler, but those baby years were a dream. We could take him to a friend's house, and he would have a great time. Same at a restaurant or a mall. There weren't many places where I needed special accommodations to have Nicholas there when he was a baby.

Marley, on the other hand, was so stressful to bring anywhere for those first three months. We had to figure out who was going to be there, if it was going to be crowded, and whether or not there was a quiet place I could take her to calm down after her inevitable freak-outs. All of that coupled with the fact that she didn't like the car and screamed the whole time didn't motivate us to do much of anything outside of our house when she was a baby. Just like the shock of Nicholas's diagnosis, Marley's behaviors as a baby caused isolation. Nicholas may have had "special needs," but Marley's needs were by far more difficult to manage.

"Special needs" doesn't always mean difficult.

Mostly, it means different. I've never met another child or student of mine who didn't have a special need in one way or the other. One student might have a terrible day if I don't chat with her in the morning and give her a little one-on-one time. Others need many physical breaks throughout the day, so I make sure I schedule them in for their benefit. Some need soothing music playing to do a quieter activity in order to better focus. Some need their coats on to feel secure in the classroom. Are these not special needs of students geared toward making them learn and function more efficiently?

We also can't ignore the "special needs" adults may have. I can easily name a few of my own. I can't teach if adults are talking in the back of my classroom. It isn't that I get a little thrown off in my lesson; it's that I can't say another word until the other adults stop. I get easily over-stimulated if there are many sources of noise happening all at once. At home, if we have people over and there is music on *and* the stove hood running, I have to make some quick changes. We all have our own sets of needs particular to us, and instead of judging them, we should try to understand them. Any other teachers or aides who know about my classroom quirk understand it and keep a really low profile while I'm teaching in order to help me be successful. Understanding the special needs of all adults and children, typically developing or otherwise, can better connect us and allow us to function at our highest level.

Now that Marley has left the baby terror stage and became an awesome toddler, I can appreciate the lessons that she's taught me already. I was meant to have Marley in my life for this reason. I needed someone to show me that my son was not the only one who needs certain things to be successful. Although my son is behind in some areas, he is way ahead in others. For that, I couldn't be prouder.

> > >

Once Nicholas transitioned into toddlerhood, he introduced us to someone we'd never met before. That person's name is Dr. Meanlips. Whenever Nicholas did something "naughty" and was told "no" he furrowed his brow, puckered his lips, tilted his head to one side while letting out a little grunt, thus earning him the nickname Dr. Meanlips. Trust me, Down syndrome doesn't make a child exempt from a terrible toddler stage; it can just mean they hit that stage a little later than their typical peers.

Before my kids were born, I fancied myself a discipline expert. I'd spent years as a babysitter and years in a classroom, all while managing way more than two kids at a time. A positive connection with the kids was the key to getting good behavior from them. My students don't behave for me because they're scared of breaking the rules; they behave for me because I take the time to establish a friendship with them. They know I have their back no matter what. I figured that if I could do this with over twenty kids at a time every year, then managing my kid would be a breeze.

What I forgot to apply to my situation was the same thing I tell parents of my students every year at conferences. Without fail, there are always some parents who come into the conference extremely nervous, waiting for the bad news they believe is inevitable. They're then shocked to hear their child is a happy and responsible member of our classroom family.

"But he's out of control at home," a parent might say. I always comfort these parents by reminding them that home is their child's safe space where they can relax and not concentrate so hard on controlling themselves. It's the place where they can let go after a long day of being an all-star classroom citizen. The same is true for teachers. After a long day of modeling acceptable behavior, I come home and roll all over the floor with my kids, not worried about how I'm carrying myself. Of course, my home is Nicholas's safe space, and he surely uses it as such.

As he got older, he started testing us. He would put his hand on something, and we would say "No, Nicholas!" After pausing, he would put his hand back on whatever we didn't want him to touch, as if to say, "Oh, so I shouldn't do this? I'm going to keep doing it then," all while transforming into Dr. Meanlips. He was trying to show us who's boss while we were trying to do the same thing. I had to start considering the strategies for discipline that I would use. Am I supposed to discipline him differently because he has Down syndrome?

One day while we were waiting for the physical therapist to arrive, Nicholas was being a little toddler tyrant and throwing his toys down the stairs when I knew he understood that I said no. We were in the process of exchanging mean lips at each other when she arrived.

"Watch out, he's being a little stinker today," I warned as she made her way up the toy-covered stairs.

"That's a really good thing," she said in a positive tone.

"Oh, yeah, okay. I'll be sure to celebrate with him later." I included a dramatic eye-roll in case she didn't catch onto my sarcasm.

"No, seriously," she continued. "He's just about to turn two, and those naughty behaviors mean he's developing right on track."

I stopped and considered this for a minute. Was she telling me that I was supposed to be happy my son was being naughty? I guess after all of this work with his development, I *should* be happy when he is on track with his peers, right? Celebrating naughty behavior wasn't something I was accustomed to.

When we're out with other people or people are over at our house, they're sometimes surprised at my strictness with Nicholas. When I set a strong boundary with him, some eyebrows go up in the room. Those eyebrows seem to say, *Wow, she seems to expect a lot out of that kid.* For me, true inclusion is not putting limits on someone just because they have a disability. You should assume people with disabilities *can* do everything anyone else can do unless you're directly informed otherwise by that individual. If more people let their baseless limits on other people go, they'll find people with disabilities more capable than they've ever been taught to believe.

As a mother, if Nicholas can understand what I want him to do or what he needs to do at that moment, then letting him off the hook simply because of his diagnosis would be a disservice to him. It relays the message that it's okay for him to not follow the rules and expectations because he has an underlying excuse. I'd hate for him to go to school and think the teacher's expectations don't apply to him because he has Down syndrome. I want him to know that he has to work harder to squash those expectations so that won't write him off in their minds. Thus far in our journey, Nicholas has shown me no sign of not being capable of understanding basic toddler rules. If I ask him to go get his jammies for bedtime, he isn't avoiding it because he has Down syndrome and doesn't understand. He's avoiding it because he doesn't want to go to bed yet! What toddler does? Assuming he doesn't understand what I'm saying would be not only a big mistake, but it would be exactly the opposite of how I want society to treat my son once he goes out into the world.

This isn't the case for everyone, but in my experience, disciplining a child with Down syndrome is no different than disciplining a typically developing child. I can't use Down syndrome as a basis for understanding him when trying to get to the core of his behaviors. Instead, I have to use what I know about him as a person *only*. I need to know what motivates Nicholas, not what motivates most kids with Down syndrome. His diagnosis is only a very small part of the bigger picture.

Down syndrome doesn't define a person.

There aren't many days that go by where he doesn't genuinely surprise me. I don't see his actions as things he does because he has Down syndrome. I see them as things he does because he's Nicholas. Nicholas is a cautious little boy. He'd never go near a staircase without making sure you're watching or can be nearby for support. He loves movies and can dance to the soundtracks all day long, acting out the dramatic scenes by moving his lips and gesturing into the air with his hands. He loves a quiet environment and favors people who calmly greet him. He loves to play with his peers. Not only do they not know he even has something called Down syndrome, they just don't care. He loves to watch his little sister succeed, and claps for her when he thinks she does something really impressive. That's who my son is. He is not a "Down syndrome kid" or "special needs kid." He's Nicholas, and he's truly one of a kind.

My perception of him has changed, but that doesn't mean other people's perceptions have. There have been many instances where people assume Nicholas is a certain way because of his diagnosis. I often remind people a lot of his behaviors are the same as those of typically developing toddlers. This is where my newfound patience has to come into play and remind me that people have to get to know Nicholas as a person. Once that happens, they can experience Nicholas's superpower, which is the ability to see life with a new perspective.

Rejoining
Society

Although it sounded much easier to extend my maternity leave indefinitely, I couldn't stay shut away forever. The old me loved my job and was passionate about it, so this new me had to go back out into the world and find that passion again. It was hard to imagine mustering the courage for such a feat when I could barely find the courage to go to the grocery store. Those first few weeks returning to my "normal" life felt like navigating a foreign city without a map.

After countless conversations and hours of research, I know it's common for new moms to have anxiety about leaving their babies for the first time. What amplified this feeling for me was that despite trying countless baby products and techniques, Nicholas would not drink his milk from a bottle. I had to return to a full-time job knowing my baby literally couldn't live without me.

Some days, my husband would put him in a highchair and attempt to cup feed him, but that was really messy and would waste the precious liquid gold that I'd worked painstakingly to stockpile. Other days, he'd drive Nicholas to my school, and I'd feed him while my students were at art, music, or gym, all while nervously watching the clock to make sure I was going to have time for a bathroom break. I'd sit in the back seat of Nick's SUV nursing our son and panicking about whether or not I'd lactated through my bra or prepared enough for the next lesson I was supposed to teach. On all of those days, I spent my lunch break pumping breastmilk at my desk while crying over a turkey sandwich.

To add to my stress, I had a classroom of kids to impress who'd just enjoyed five months with their substitute teacher, whom they loved and adored. Not only did I have to mask my pain and be the teacher they'd hoped to have, but I felt I had to go above and beyond. Relationships have everything to do with success in the classroom, and I couldn't let my students meet this depressed version of myself that was only just starting to fade away. The effort exerted for me to merely be "myself" was exhausting. Even with all of those factors in play, the main source of my anxiety had nothing to do with Nicholas or my students.

The real reason I was nervous was that I finally had to tell people about Nicholas out loud, in person, and on purpose. Until that point, I'd treated it as a secret to be kept. I had no idea how to start. Was I supposed to bring it up when people welcomed me back? That wasn't right, was it? If they asked how my baby was, was I supposed to say, "Oh he's great. He has Down syndrome, by the way, but he's great." No one was going to outright ask me, so I couldn't wait for it to come up organically. I'd hidden it thus far because I didn't want people to judge him or worse, feel sorry for him. The thought of receiving pity in any way left a pit in my stomach. I couldn't face my colleagues who I'd only known for a year and be brave.

It just so happened that I returned to work a month before World Down Syndrome Day (WDSD). WDSD is a global awareness event that happens every year on March 21st. The date, 3/21, represents the three copies of the twenty-first chromosome. I casually mentioned doing some sort of celebration with my class to my colleagues in the office one day, and they ran with the idea. A teacher I didn't know well at the time made amazing T-shirts, and we sold them to the staff to raise money for our local Down syndrome achievement center. Other teachers asked me for resources so they could take time out of their days to teach their classes about Down syndrome. The student council even did a fundraiser, allowing students to rock their crazy socks to support the cause. When the day came, I couldn't believe how many members of the staff purchased a T-shirt and how many students had crazy mismatched socks to celebrate the holiday. We were able to donate over seven hundred dollars.

Since then, our celebration has grown to be district wide. Something I wasn't even going to mention to anyone turned into a huge awareness campaign. I was so happy with the outpouring of support from people who didn't know me well at all. They only knew I was on their team and wanted to show support. My fear of passing colleagues in the hall faded fast, and I always welcomed an opportunity to brag about my son.

I've found people are more supportive than I originally expected. There are going to be ups and downs as you return to your "life as usual," but in my experience, if you simply ask for support from others, you'll most likely receive it, so don't be afraid. I *was* too afraid to ask but received it anyway, so being direct can only help you even more.

There were some new menu items I didn't have on my plate before Nicholas, such as therapy sessions, meetings with service coordinators, IEP meetings, evaluations, and countless other things. Fitting them in at all was hard and understanding the intricacies of them was harder. There were also the many confusing interactions I had with others concerning Nicholas's diagnosis I wasn't prepared for. The next set of lessons I'm sharing have to do with returning to the real world after the diagnosis while navigating all the new experiences that came with it.

Lesson 7

There are people out there waiting to help.

This is hard. I have no one to call. My friends don't understand my situation. Too many people are giving me too much advice. I don't know where to start. Help.

Being the mother of a child with special needs doesn't come with an instruction manual. If it does, I surely didn't get my copy at check-in, and someone has some explaining to do. The laws and regulations concerning the rights of people with special needs can be difficult to understand, especially since they seem to change constantly. Many people had suggestions for me about what to do next, but it contradicted what I'd been told by doctors up until that point. Luckily, there are places throughout the country that exist to help parents through the various processes they need to best support their children. From making sure you're signing up for respite funds to attending IEP meetings alongside you, these people are meant to act as an advocate for both you *and* your child.

They can even speak up on your behalf when you don't feel experienced enough to do so. Since there are federal laws around people with special needs, these centers exist in more places than you'd think.

Our town is not somewhere I would think to find a special needs advocacy center. We live in a town on a lake that is highly residential and where the people are used to driving forty minutes to a major city just to go to a doctor's appointment or out to dinner. I was shocked to find how close my advocacy center was. Coincidentally, I'd found it two years prior by accident.

While I was getting my master's degree in childhood education, long before Nicholas, I was given the assignment to interview a parent of a person with special needs about their experiences with special education in public schools. I didn't have many contacts where I lived at the time and asked my professor for help. She was a former special education teacher, so she knew a few parents who could lend me some of their time.

She introduced me to Theresa. Not only was she the mother of a man with autism who'd finished his journey through the school system, but she was also the leader of an organization that helped support parents of children with special needs. As I listened to the final directions of my GPS and pulled into her office parking lot, my heart rate quickened. I was going somewhere I'd never been to meet someone I'd never met, and it made me nervous. But, like every mom of a child with special needs I've met during my journey, she welcomed me with open arms and gave me as much time as I needed.

My nerves washed away as we chit-chatted in her office. As it turned out, she was a graduate of my former high school, which was two hours away from where we sat. It was cool to have that in common. With the culture of my high school being so centered around school pride, being a Johnson City Wildcat sort of sticks with people. So, after talking about our favorite restaurants in our hometown, I interviewed her in her office, completed my assignment, aced it, and honestly never thought I'd see her again. Even so, I had a weird sense that I wanted to keep in touch with her but didn't seem to have a good enough reason to maintain contact.

Two short years later, when I was finally out of my cloud of depression long enough to look for support, I thought of Theresa. I remembered enjoying our conversation and felt comfortable reaching out to her. This meant a lot because I wasn't talking to *anyone* yet. I remembered from our interview that she helped people with the "what do I do now" questions they have concerning their children and made sure the *parents* had what they needed, and not just their kids. When I contacted her, she was quick to congratulate me on the birth of my son. I couldn't sense even a hint of condolence in her voice, which was refreshing. She also informed me her office had moved. Not only had it moved closer to where I lived, but it moved to my street. A street with nothing on it but some houses and a tiny post office also now included a place that could help me figure out this new life.

The comfort of Theresa's new office moving to my street caused the first feeling of believing that I was meant for this path. After months of thinking *why me?* and *how is this real?* this was a special moment. Many of the moms I've connected with shared a similar sentiment of feeling way too ill-equipped to take on such a unique parenting job at first. This first spark of hope meant the world to me, confirming that I could handle these challenges, and that maybe I *was* built for this.

This group gave me the tools to be able to sign up for early intervention services to help with Nicholas's development, respite funds to help provide money for childcare, and many other programs that I didn't know existed. There were more benefits available to me than I would've ever expected to find on my own, and talking to people who navigate these benefits for a living made it easy. Both Theresa and her colleague Erica are parents of special children, so talking to them about all of the difficult feelings I had was a lot easier than talking to parents of typically developing kids. They knew where I was coming from. When I went for my initial meeting, I brought my husband and Nicholas, got myself reacquainted with them both, and left feeling like I had someone to call if I had any questions for the first time since Nicholas was born. I recommend becoming closely acquainted with your local advocates not only because they're helpful, but because you might find yourself sobbing in their office as I'd done a couple of months later.

I've always assumed that everyone who works in the business of special needs would have the best interests of the individuals in mind at all times. To me, that seemed like a no-brainer. As a teacher, I was already used to being an advocate for children and enjoyed that part of my job the most. I figured I'd see the same thing when it came to people who work with children with special needs. This seems like an area where you have to be passionate to choose it as a career path. I found out that this was not the case for everyone. Just like any job, there are people in this industry who might get burnt out and allow that burnout to cause frustration. Thankfully, I had Theresa and Erica on my side when I needed backup.

When you sign your child up for services, you are assigned a "service coordinator." This person is to be a liaison between you and your various therapy providers. He or she will also check in periodically to make sure everything is going all right. One time, I asked one of my early service coordinators if we'd be eligible for certain benefits I'd heard about through another parent. She gave a little laugh with a look on her face that said *yeah, right, that'll never happen.* She explained that a lot of people get denied these particular benefits, and there was no way that Nicholas would be eligible for them. She told me trying would be a waste of time. Her immediate dismissal of my request without looking into it rubbed me the wrong way, but I thought she'd know best since she'd been in this business longer than I had. I explained to her that I was going to seek help from the group down the street that I had found, and she still advised against it. I almost listened to her, too.

When she left, I had someone come watch Nicholas so I could go down the street and ask the advocacy group about it. Erica, whose desk was nearest to the door, asked, "You're Mary, right?" When I said yes, she told me my service coordinator had just called and instructed them to not help me in filling out the paperwork to apply for the benefits I sought because she thought I should figure it out for myself. Erica quickly followed that by saying she started the paperwork anyway because their job was to advocate for families. This was the kind of thing they lived for, helping parents when the cards were stacked against them.

I couldn't respond right away because I was immediately overcome with emotion. I'd already suffered the trauma of the diagnosis and was completely new at this. I was finally coming out of it to explore my options. I was uncomfortable with the conversation that I'd just had at my house, but also so happy Erica had stuck up for me before I'd even set foot in the door. All I wanted was the best for my son, as everyone wants for their children. I parked myself in a waiting room chair and sobbed into my hands. I couldn't believe there were people out there that got in the way of me seeking help for my son and actively making phone calls to prevent me from getting help. Theresa and Erica listened to my frustrations, and I felt comfortable letting go in front of them since they'd been so welcoming to me before. They've had their fair share of frustrating experiences in their parenting journeys and welcomed the opportunity to help me with mine.

Actively seek the agencies that exist to help parents.
If I hadn't known Theresa from my college assignment, I'm not sure how I would've even started the process of looking for resources for Nicholas. I was so fortunate to be in a situation of personally knowing the people I was reaching out to. Though I don't know what it would've been like to push past the boundaries of comfort to find more information, I urge new parents to find these people as soon as possible. They could be the people in your corner when you feel alone in the fight.

Let fact-checking be the new normal.
From then on, and even to this day, I question every bit of advice I get from any professional. Doctors, teachers, therapists, or anyone else who gives me advice about my son has to give me time to check that information with other sources. The laws change so much in this area that those people might not even have the most updated information and give you advice with the best intentions. Be up to date on policy changes and triple check information regularly. Even if the source of the information is one you trust, it doesn't hurt to look into it yourself. Also, if you were wondering, Nicholas received those benefits I'd sought without a hiccup.

This was yet another experience since Nicholas had been born where a wound of mine was healed by a community of people with a shared experience. Adding the very best resources to my community was an important step, while also being on high alert for misinformation.

Lesson 8

I am an expert member of my child's team.

I've always been a lifelong rule-follower, so it isn't exactly shocking that I grew up to be a teacher. As a student, I was always on time, I always had my work done, and I had my school subjects organized by color. When we dealt with Nicholas's diagnosis, I went into student mode. I allowed everyone to teach me about what I was going through instead of paying close attention to what I experienced for myself. Whatever the doctors said was, to me, regarded as undeniable truth. If I learned something new from someone who worked in special education, I viewed that information as concrete fact. I figured all these people must know more than me since I'd never had a chance to properly prepare for this job. The submissive, ever-obedient student came forward, and the leader in me sat the bench.

Finding out that information that came directly from doctors was inaccurate or outdated was as shocking a blow as the diagnosis itself. It caused me to yet again doubt everything I thought I knew before. I no longer see doctors the way I always had. It wasn't until I became a teacher that I realized my teachers didn't know everything as I thought they'd had when I was growing up. Instead of all-knowing wizards of medicine, I now see doctors as humans who can make mistakes. If I can make mistakes in my profession, I am sure they can too. That doesn't mean they're bad at their jobs. It means it can be difficult to keep track of the intricate world of special needs.

Two doctors and a nurse told me in the very beginning that I wouldn't be able to engage in early intervention services with Nicholas until his developmental delays were more significant. In other words, he had to be "more behind" his typical peers to qualify. They also said if I tried to get the services and was denied, it would take a long time for us to be eligible to reapply, so the time had to be just right. This made us even less motivated to try and get the ball rolling. Why risk getting denied, right? I was happy to hear he wasn't behind enough yet to be eligible and allowed that to be the truth. At the time, I still believed there were varying degrees of Down syndrome and thought *hey, maybe his isn't so bad.* Even reflecting on my past ignorance now makes me cringe.

When I finally found the advocacy center, they informed me that people born with Down syndrome are considered "automatic qualifiers" for early intervention because being behind in development is a part of the diagnosis. In theory, he could've left the hospital as a newborn and gone directly to a therapy session. Since the doctors told me otherwise, I didn't see the need to investigate it further. As a result, Nicholas wasn't enrolled in early intervention until he was five months old. Meanwhile, he was five months old and could not make a fist on his own. I'm still mad at myself for being complacent and missing out on five months of professional help for my child.

I always see Nicholas's true potential come out in his therapy sessions and can't help but wonder what difference those first five months could've made. Right after signing Nicholas up for an evaluation, my rock star advocates called both doctors to correct their information to protect other families from that mistake.

There was another instance when a colleague who I'd worked with in my year of student teaching gave me some advice I had almost blindly followed assuming she would know better. She'd worked in special education for years and was highly regarded in her school district. We'd kept in touch after student teaching thanks to social media, and she would send me encouraging messages from time to time when she would see pictures of Nicholas pop up on her newsfeed.

One day, one of those messages heeded more like a warning. She seemed shocked that even though Nicholas was one and a half and non-verbal, I hadn't gotten him some sort of communicative device. I immediately spiraled into the fear that the people I trusted with the fate of my son were wrong again. Had I wasted more time in a state of complacency?

I quickly reached out to each of our four therapists, and they all said the same thing: if he were *not* showing signs of understanding the language presented to him and using his sign language in context, he would've been issued a communicative device. It was less about speech and more about language. The speech therapist also said it was a good sign he was attempting to make the sounds and didn't want him relying on a device to communicate if he was showing growth verbally. She worried that if he'd gotten too comfortable using a device, he would stop trying to make the sounds because he simply wouldn't feel he needed to.

This put my mind at ease, but I was still skeptical. I didn't want to listen to the wrong source. After mulling over it for days, I realized my colleague's comment was based on age, not developmental ability. She'd never even met Nicholas and was basing her professional opinion on other kids with Down syndrome she'd worked with during her career. I had to remember that our decisions had to be made based on what we knew about *our* child, not other children with Down syndrome. Between the therapist's advice and the fact that I didn't want to ruin Nicholas's momentum by giving him a device, I let go of the whole idea. I might not have known as much about adaptive learning as she did, but I did know more about Nicholas.

These instances didn't cause me to stop trusting the opinions of the professionals in Nicholas's life. Instead, I started trusting my role as his mother more. Down syndrome is tricky. There's a wide range of abilities and characteristics that each person can have. To know what's best for a child, you need to *know* the child and work with them regularly.

Even when situations cause me to doubt my choices with Nicholas, I try to see them as learning experiences. I gained new knowledge in both scenarios and learned new options for my son. The more information I can gather, the more prepared I can feel for the job of being Nicholas's mother and advocate. Doctors may have more information about medicine, and special education teachers might have more information about adaptive devices, but I have the valuable information that ties it all together: I know Nicholas. Once I saw myself as a fellow expert, I was able to step back into a leadership role.

As his in-home expert, I had the job of enrolling him in preschool, which meant scheduling his first-ever IEP meeting. An IEP, or individualized education plan, is a document created by the parents, teachers, therapists, and anyone else who has a stake in a child's life. This legal document exists to ensure that children with special needs get any adaptations they require to obtain a fair education. I was fortunate enough to have the background knowledge of attending IEP meetings in the past as a teacher. Parents had the power, and they could suggest anything they thought would help their child. Parents had the ability to table a meeting if they couldn't reach an agreement with the school. What I didn't know was what it felt like to actually be the parent at an IEP meeting.

To say I was nervous about Nicholas going to preschool would be the understatement of the century. There was so much to worry about, and the stress kept me up at night. He was to start preschool in the middle of the COVID-19 pandemic. He was going to be dropped off at a building filled with strangers without me being allowed inside. He was going to ride the bus to his babysitter's house for the first time in his life. The idea of any of these things scaring him for even a second made me sick.

So, when it came down to his first IEP meeting, I had a list of questions ready to go. When I made that list, I thought about what an ideal school day would look like for Nicholas based on what I knew about him and considered what could be done to make that ideal school day happen. I wanted to consider every outcome so I could be prepared.

In virtual meetings, I take the people who are well-lit more seriously. It's one of the weird ways I measure people. To me, the smartest people make sure their faces are clearly visible because they'll likely have a lot to say. This also shows that they have a level of planning and preparedness I always appreciate. So, I sat down for his IEP meeting facing the window so everyone in attendance knew I meant business.

Don't be afraid to speak up.

I'm happy to report that the very first IEP meeting went smoothly. I had one major concern about speech therapy being suggested for only three days a week, but when I opened my mouth to express this concern the speech therapist in attendance asked if it could be raised to five days a week. After seeing how far he'd come, I was excited about how fast he could make progress with so many therapy sessions mixed with school and daily peer interaction.

In this first meeting, I had no real reason to raise concerns or ask for further information. However, as a teacher who attends IEP meetings for students, I can't help but wonder if parents are too nervous to ask questions or request clarification. I recommend any parent or guardian who attends a meeting on a child's behalf take notes and make sure they understand all the education lingo being presented to them. Even though the meeting made me a little nervous, it wasn't the true source of my anxiety. What stressed me out the most couldn't be solved in an IEP meeting. I was afraid of a difficult transition, and Nicholas crying for me every day at drop off.

Nicholas would eventually get used to school, and it would probably be harder for me than it was for him, but I still worried. For a couple of days, I resigned myself to the idea that it was going to be hard, and that was that. If I couldn't think of how to make this transition better while not being allowed inside the school ahead of time, who could? Then I remembered I was not the *only* expert on Nicholas's team, and he was about to get an entirely new team. I reached out to the director of the preschool, who gave me an amazing suggestion. She told me she would send me pictures of what would be Nicholas's classroom and all of his teachers so I could turn them into a book. I did just that, and we read the book every single night in the weeks before his first day at school. I'll never know if it truly helped Nicholas, but it definitely made me feel better. Within two days, Nicholas loved school and drop off became a breeze. Well, a breeze for him, anyway.

First day of
PRESCHOOL
2020-2021

In the second week of school, right when Nicholas was getting comfortable in his new grueling schedule, he was sent home with a cough. Since coughing was a symptom of COVID-19, it was their policy to require him to get a COVID test before he would be able to return. I was so grateful my husband immediately picked him up and took him for the test because the thought of having to restrain him for a nose swab in the second week of school didn't sound like it would help my anxiety. The turnaround time for results was two days, causing him to miss those days of school.

In those two days, I started to worry about what his future at school would look like as long as the pandemic was going on. I understood the precautions that the school had taken, but due to Down syndrome, Nicholas has smaller tubes in his respiratory system than his typical peers. His low muscle tone also makes it more difficult for him to clear mucus from his nose and throat. As a result, Nicholas coughs all the time. I started to wonder if would he be sent home regularly to get a COVID test, having to wait two days every time? How much schooling would he miss because of this? What if this pandemic lasted for years? This was Nicholas's opportunity to level the playing field before entering kindergarten. I had to be proactive to ensure he wouldn't miss school regularly simply because he is destined to cough more than the average kid. Whenever I consider whether or not a decision is fair for him, I wonder whether or not the situation is a direct consequence of having Down syndrome. Since common identifiers of Down syndrome caused his "symptoms," I had a case.

Approach conflicts as a problem solver.

Whenever we need to make any kind of customer complaint, my husband makes me call the company because he thinks I can "give them the business" and have the conversation go in our favor. However, I didn't want to have that kind of rapport with my son's school. I didn't want to be the parent they dreaded talking to on the phone. I work in education too, and I wanted to work more as a collaborator than a complainer.

This was a particularly tricky situation because all three parties—our family, the school, and the pediatrician—had reasonable concerns. The preschool couldn't turn a blind eye to what could be the symptom of a highly contagious virus, the doctor's office couldn't write a note that dismissed symptoms of a highly contagious virus, and my son couldn't be turned away from school simply because he has Down syndrome. His school also happened to be the only inclusive preschool program within a reasonable driving distance. Switching schools was out of the question.

I reached out to both the director of the preschool and my pediatrician. I communicated clearly and professionally that although I understood that no one wanted to disregard a symptom of coronavirus, something had to give when it came to my son's frequent coughing. I didn't ask anyone if it was okay. I didn't apologize. My son deserved the education all of his peers were getting and I wasn't going to let anything get in the way of that. The student in me was gone, replaced by the leader my son needed.

In a few back-and-forth phone calls, the three of us were able to come to an agreement. I would closely monitor Nicholas's health every morning before he would go to school. If his cough was mixed with any other symptoms, I would keep him home and monitor further. Even though he was only sent home for his cough that first time, I was proud of myself for being proactive and ensuring that it wouldn't become a regular occurrence. I no longer allowed the rules to be the rules and chose to dig deeper into those rules so my son could have the best opportunities available. I was so thankful for the collaboration we established, because it's helped us solve other issues since then.

Know the IEP inside and out.

If you focus on one thing to be a true expert in, make it the IEP. The IEP is a legal document that teachers and anyone else working with your child must follow. Because of the importance of this document, it is detailed and long. What I do is create a bulleted cheat sheet that shows me clearly what the school and teachers will implement in order to best support Nicholas. I try to never put myself in a situation where I'm not sure what's on my son's IEP so I'm prepared to make changes if I feel the need to bring up a concern.

Doctors, therapists, teachers, school directors, and many other people will help my son along the way, but they're not the only experts on what is best for him. I'm an expert too, because I know him best. As soon as I regarded myself as such, I felt more comfortable and confident in the daily workings of Nicholas's care. Even so, no one becomes an expert without putting in the work, so making sure I'm as informed as possible is crucial.

Do the studying, but when the time comes, be the leader, not the student.

Lesson 9

Medical surprises happen.

I held my one-year-old son on my lap, pressing a clear oxygen mask over his mouth and nose. The doctor had just left the room to get the opinion of another doctor, leaving the door open behind him. Nicholas, who usually protested anything touching his face, lay in my arms with his eyes closed, masked in the fog of the breathing treatment. The loud hum of the machine made it so I couldn't hear anything else and had to resist the urge to yell, "Someone please hurry!"

When they returned, they looked at Nicholas, talked back and forth for a moment, and the second doctor quickly vanished again. The first came a little closer so I could hear him better.

"We're going to call you an ambulance."

> > >

Before that day, I never understood what people meant when they said they were paralyzed with fear. I felt welded to the chair and wondered if my legs would work well enough to stand when the

EMTs arrived. I weighed every possibility I knew of. I'd read all the blogs and followed so many social media accounts. I knew how common it was for kids with Down syndrome to have medical surprises, but I couldn't wrap my head around Nicholas needing an ambulance. How could this be happening to my perfect boy?

Apparently, I spoke with other doctors and nurses after that. Apparently, my husband took my car keys and moved my car before we left after I'd barely acknowledged his arrival. Apparently, I signed a bunch of paperwork. I don't remember any of those things. My tunnel vision was focused on my son lying on a gurney meant for an adult, strapped down with seat belts and hooked up to an oxygen mask. There was my little boy in his fuzzy moose sweatshirt, too weak to keep his eyes open, about to be installed into a speeding metal box. The only thing that felt natural for me was how quickly I hopped into the ambulance with him.

I sat in a seat close enough for me to be able to help support his head while the paramedic examined him. As I stretched over, I looked over my shoulder for Nick, who followed us in his red Ford Explorer. If the roles were reversed, I would've never been able to keep up with the ambulance, but Nick was meant for this job. Years later, when the kids and I were in a car accident, I called 911 first, then Nick. Nick arrived before the police. He's always been a pretty great first responder.

"Here, put this on." The medic handed me a surgical mask after putting one on himself. "I'm about to administer something that could increase our heart rates."

"I'm pregnant, is this safe for me?"

"As long as you have the mask on, yes."

I put the mask over my face and peeked out the back window. I wanted to give Nick a thumbs up so the mask didn't make him panic, but he was gone. It wasn't like him to care about the speed limit in an emergency. I started to worry about where he could possibly be.

"Lift your butt off the seat," the medic said as I turned back around. I didn't ask questions; I just stood up like a surfer catching a wave. As soon as I did, we hit a bump that would've sent me to the roof of the ambulance had I still been sitting on the bench. The long journey to the nearest children's hospital no longer felt so scary. If these guys knew every bump in the road for a forty-five-minute stretch of highway, then they knew what they were doing.

When we finally pulled into the ambulance drop-off area, Nick was already standing there. Instead of falling behind as I'd feared, he'd sped ahead so he wouldn't miss anything. We were quickly ushered into a check-in room and drilled with questions. One of those questions was: "Does he have any illnesses other than Down syndrome?"

I wanted to scream that Down syndrome wasn't an illness, but I was too numb to do so and could only muster a "no" while basking in the disappointment of that particular mistake being made by a medical professional.

We were moved to a room where only sick and possibly contagious children were examined before assessing whether or not to admit them. At the time, I thought we were just getting special treatment since the patient in question was only a baby, but actually the staff was afraid of spreading whatever they thought he might have, as we learned from their mumblings to one another. The emergency room started filling up, and stretchers were lined up with sick children in the hallways. I was thankful we were in a private area but wondered what that could mean for Nicholas. The nurses told us it would be a while before a decision was made on whether or not to admit Nicholas, so we took turns snuggling him on the bed while watching a Tom Hanks movie marathon on

AMC. The movies *Castaway*, *The Green Mile*, and *The Da Vinci Code* played on repeat and acted as our clock for the days to come.

As the chubby version of Tom Hanks's character in *Castaway* was enjoying his Christmas Eve dinner, a team of nurses came in to put an IV into Nicholas's arm. My husband and I scrambled to make this as quick and painless as possible. We put his favorite show on a cellphone and held it in front of him. We directed his attention away from his arm. We told him repeatedly how brave he was. What I learned shortly after that was Nicholas has an extremely high threshold for pain. Instead of the screaming I'd expected, he just turned to me and frowned. He was more annoyed with the cast-like device they installed onto his arm to prevent him from touching the needle than of the needle itself.

We were seen by every doctor who was working that night and became pros at answering the "So, when did this all start?" question asked by every single one of them. I'd tell my part about how the night before he was up with a cough. Nick would then jump in and explain that during the day, he seemed lethargic and uncomfortable. Then I'd jump back in to talk about how I picked Nicholas up from the babysitter, noticed his red spots and labored breathing, and rushed him to the pediatrician. It turned into a rehearsed skit with how many times we had to recite it. Each time, the doctors looked up at the TV and made some comments about the movie. Something about this movie being on struck a chord with everyone who was working there. I mean, everyone knows *Castaway*.

After Nicholas was given medicine to reduce his fever and was done getting hooked to all of his monitors, the FedEx plane crashed, leaving Tom Hanks alone on the island with no one but a dirty volleyball to talk to. Similarly, we wouldn't see the doctors again until Tom Hanks's rescue.

About two hours later, they'd been monitoring Nicholas's progress enough to make a decision about admitting him. By then, Tom Hanks's wife had to choose between her new husband and her scrawny island husband. Each doctor who visited shook their heads at the TV in disapproval. Even the tech who helped us move to our second room scoffed. "Oh no, I hate this part. I can't believe she didn't wait for him. It was only seven years. Come on, lady, have some loyalty. Oh, by the way, we're pretty crowded tonight, and you're going to be sharing a room for a while."

Until this point, we were pretty comfortable in the large, private exam room. We weren't thrilled to have to share a room but knew it was another small child and figured it wouldn't be so bad.

As it turned out, just as *Castaway* ended, so did our luck.

> > >

"This is fucking disgusting. No wonder babies fucking die."

These were the first words we heard from the mother of the other child when she saw Nicholas. The positivity we were trying to uphold started its downfall from there. Her daughter wasn't a baby. Did she think mine was going to die? What was making him "fucking disgusting"? His unknown illness? His Down syndrome? Of all the rooms to end up in, this one was ours.

Sure, her frustrations weren't completely crazy. You should've seen this hospital room. It was made for one patient, but there were two beds, two cribs, and only a thin curtain in between. The crib on our side and the bed on their side were almost touching through the curtain. When we realized we would have to stay there overnight, we knew things were about to get a little uncomfortable.

Our roommates had a little girl with asthma. Since Nicholas was also having trouble breathing, I could relate to the panic they felt. Instead of recognizing their feelings, they instead took their frustrations out on our little guy, who could do nothing but lay there and sleep.

During *The Green Mile*, when Tom Hanks was suffering from a urinary tract infection, the mother on the other side of the room called whoever would listen to say she had to have her daughter in a room with a "disgusting sick kid who probably has a ton of things wrong with him." She followed up most phone calls with, "My daughter better not catch anything that kid has."

Even though we'd never met, I felt truly betrayed by her. Deep down, we were the same. We were both moms who wanted one thing: to have our kids breathe oxygen without a struggle. To most moms, this might not seem like a lot to ask. We have this unique shared experience that should've bonded us, but her fear and ignorance about Down syndrome ruined that.

For the rest of the night, we sat and listened to her negative comments from the stretcher we had to share while Nicholas slept in his hospital crib. Her painful words were way louder than the cast of *The Green Mile*, but she was just another uninformed person we didn't know how to approach. For all we knew, she thought her daughter could catch Down syndrome. I'm thankful Nicholas was too small to be hurt by her words. If he were older and understood what she was saying, she would've had a lot of explaining to do.

To distract us from the negativity, we decided to scour some trusted internet sources to try to figure out what Nicholas *could* have. The memories of being told incorrect things from medical professionals were still fresh, and we wanted to at least have some ideas in the back of our minds when we were approached by doctors. The days of accepting the first diagnosis were long gone, and I wanted to be as informed as possible. We learned, and the doctor confirmed, that it's common for children with Down syndrome to have small tubes throughout their respiratory systems. So, a small cold could turn into a big problem for some people like it does for Nicholas. However, they weren't convinced it was just a cold, so we hunkered down for a long night of uncomfortable sleep and awkward walks to the bathroom.

> > >

As the sun came up, AMC advertised another night of the Tom Hanks movie marathon. We overheard that we would be moving to the children's hospital upstairs. Honestly, they could have moved us to the coat closet upstairs and it would've been preferable to listening to a stranger insult my son all night.

Nicholas's hospital crib/jail cell was on wheels, so we packed up our things and followed the staff as they rolled him out of the room and down the hallway. As we made our way to the new location, I realized this was the first time Nicholas's health had stopped him from doing something fun. That weekend, we were supposed to be out of town visiting an aquarium with him. He loved our small fish tank, and we couldn't wait to see his reaction to a huge aquarium with thousands of fish. We told this to the nurses on our way up, who'd already given us condolences for a horrible night with our former roommates. Apparently, they'd had a horrible night because of them too.

While we chatted, the hallway decor went from a generic beige to a newly remodeled back-lit solar system. The smells changed from gross hospital smells to clean hotel room smells. I got the feeling our new room was going to be no coat closet. When we got there, I couldn't believe it. We had a huge private room with a new flat screen, big bathroom with a shower, and couch that folded out into a full-size bed. If we were going to be in a constant state of fear and anxiety about Nicholas, at least now we could be comfortable.

Everyone who entered our room from then on had full protective gear on. Surgical masks, gloves, paper smocks, the works. After seeing that even the food service person was fully clad, I asked the nurse, "Are we in danger?"

"We aren't sure what he has yet, but whatever it is, you probably have it by now anyway. Your bodies might just be better at fighting it. But while we wait for his tests to come back, I brought him a little present."

She pulled out a small fish-tank toy that was filled with real water that bubbled and moved the fish all around. She'd remembered that he was missing out on the aquarium and brought the aquarium to him. There's truly nothing like the care and consideration of a nurse. Nicholas loved looking at it, as I'm sure he was sick of Tom Hanks, and watching him enjoy the fish dampened the fear that we all might have some sort of dangerous sickness.

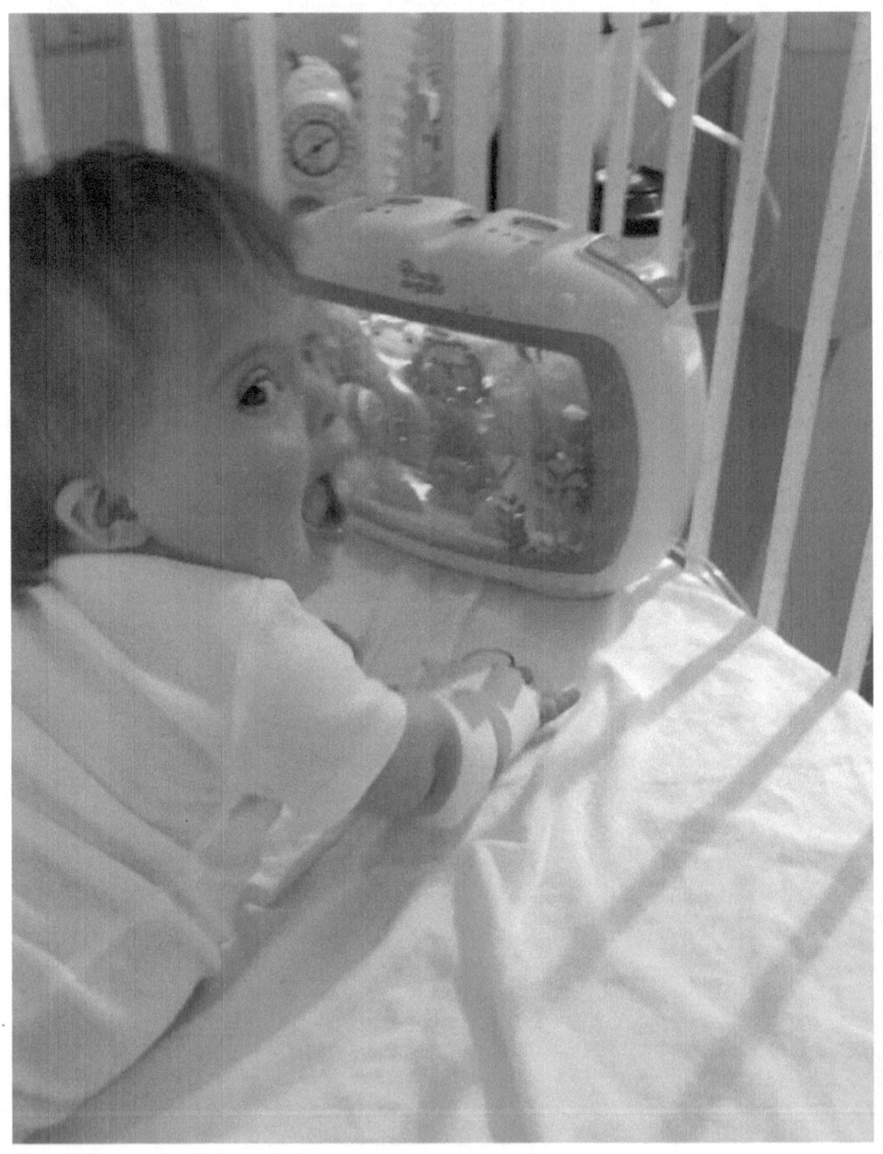

As it turned out, it wasn't just a small cold made worse by tiny respiratory tubes. On the third day of our stay, we found out that Nicholas had a coronavirus. This was almost two years *before* the COVID-19 pandemic, and we were told that "coronavirus" was a big word for a certain kind of cold. I think they may have undersold it, because years later when all of the panic ensued surrounding coronavirus, Nick and I figured it wasn't a big deal. We certainly didn't expect the world to shut down. Nicholas's strain of coronavirus was also paired with bronchiolitis, and what they suspected to be the beginning signs of asthma. We haven't seen signs of asthma since but are certainly on high alert for the signs now.

At the end of the third day, Nicholas was feeling well enough to be sent home. Nicholas and I were wheeled to the lobby together since he was too small to sit in the wheelchair on his own. As the nurse pushed us, I noticed that we weren't going in the direction I thought we should be. Wasn't she supposed to be taking us to the exit where Nick was waiting? We turned a corner, and right in front of us was a huge fish tank in a lobby we didn't know about. The nurse wanted Nicholas to still see some real fish that weekend since she knew he missed out on his big trip. We went right up close to it, and his eyes tracked the fish around the tank as he smiled from ear to ear. Her kindness toward him erased the cruelty of the woman we'd shared the hospital room with two nights before.

After driving an hour back home, we bathed Nicholas and took turns showering the hospital smell off ourselves. Sitting on the couch with our wet hair and fresh sweats, we talked about how lucky we were, and how that experience could've been so much worse. We also knew that once our second baby came, it would be impossible for us both to spend a weekend at the hospital with Nicholas. Someone would have to stay behind. So, we pondered what we could've done differently, and what we could do in the future to make sure these surprises don't completely destroy us.

We came up with a few ideas.

Be Proactive.

That third copy of the twenty-first chromosome can cause a wide range of medical surprises. Even when I think I've read about all of them, I'll read something I've never heard of before. Our pediatrician has been amazing when it comes to helping us be proactive. He schedules us to see specialists regularly and monitors his health closely. We even have blood drawn every few months to check for Leukemia or anything else that can occur with kids who have Down syndrome. I'm also constantly looking for new information to read so I can stay as current as possible with my own knowledge. My hope is to limit the number of times that medical hiccups stop Nicholas from doing fun kid things.

I have to say, we've been very fortunate thus far when it comes to Nicholas's health. Many parents I communicate with through my blog are not as lucky and have to endure challenges that I couldn't imagine. When I hear these stories, I always wonder what could be in store for Nicholas. Even though the worries will always exist in the back of my mind, I try to only focus on the fact that he is enjoying a healthy and happy childhood.

Make the best of it.

That weekend seemed like an eternity to us, but we know it could've been much longer. The hospital is famously not a very fun place to hang out. Luckily, I was with my husband who helped lighten our spirits and pass the time. When my worry was starting to show a little too much, he would redirect us to a movie or game. As scary as it was, I have some nice memories of those nights in the hospital, and the experience has made me unafraid of having to endure similar visits in the future. Medical surprises will happen, and now I'm ready to hide my fear and make sure my son can have some worry-free entertainment.

That weekend, we also saw insensitivity toward Nicholas because of his diagnosis firsthand. Our roommate's comments pushed me to share the medical side of Down syndrome with the readers of my blog hoping that the more people know, the less likely they'll be to make snap judgments about innocent babies. Those were by far the worst intentional comments we've heard thus far, but we've since learned that not everyone makes these comments with hate in their hearts. The best we can do is continue to share knowledge and hope to dispel any ignorance or fear toward people with Down syndrome.

Lesson 10

Most people aren't ignorant on purpose.

When we were first told about Nicholas's diagnosis, I couldn't help myself from worrying about the future possibility of someone making fun of him. The thought of him feeling isolated from his peers crushed me. At the time of writing this book, my son isn't old enough to be in that situation yet, but our experience with ignorance surrounding Down syndrome didn't end with the woman in the emergency room. Even so, I figured that unless we were coming into direct contact with people then the topic would never even come up. Never in a million years did I expect to be approached by so many people who wanted to comment on his "condition" or "situation" as many times as I have.

The first time it happened was in the Walmart parking lot. A woman watched as I clumsily transferred Nicholas's car seat from the stroller into the back seat of my car. On that particular day, I'd called in sick to work because the doctor wanted to give Nicholas a re-check after we'd both been sick. I hadn't planned on being out in public at all, but on the way home I remembered that I was almost out of baby aspirin. Clad in sweatpants, with a loose bun flopping back and forth on top of my head, I tried to quickly get him into the car to avoid the drizzling rain, but the lock had gotten stuck. From the woman's perspective, I'm sure my entire look screamed "new mom."

I'd just gotten the car seat to latch into the base when I heard her say, "How old is he?"

I shut the door to the back seat and turned toward her. "Almost eight months!"

"Oh, my goodness, honey! You need to start getting him out of that car seat and carrying him around!"

Of course, she didn't know he was behind in development. She also didn't know how badly I wished I could just hold him on my hip to run into the store and grab something. She couldn't have known that I longed for the day I could leave the heavy car seat in the car and plop Nicholas into the shopping cart seat. All she had was her background knowledge on developmental milestones, and I'm willing to bet that knowledge didn't include kids with special needs. To her, I was treating a big kid like a newborn. I'm sure she was trying to help the hot mess she saw in the parking lot, but it was the first time that someone's comments gave me a sinking feeling in my gut.

"Soon!" was all that I could say while feigning fake excitement and loading the folded stroller into the hatch. I got into my car and drove off like I'd just robbed the place.

As I pondered what had happened on the ride home, I realized that even though her comment wasn't directly Down syndrome related, it had given me that defensive feeling deep down. I wished I could go back and tell her it isn't polite to make assumptions about people's children but didn't even feel knowledgeable enough to have an argument like that. I didn't know when typically developing kids started sitting up. I didn't know when the average baby with Down syndrome started to, either. It threw me for a loop, and I was nowhere near prepared for when the comments would be directly related to Down syndrome.

Sure, he wasn't sitting up yet. Do you know what he *was* doing? He was being laid down for bed every night and lulling himself to sleep within five minutes. He woke me up in the mornings with coos instead of cries. He was agreeable wherever we went in public and never gave us a hard time. I focused on those amazing positives and promised myself that I would mentally prepare for interactions like this in the future, thinking it would be a long time until it happened again.

As it turned out, I only had to wait a few months.

The following summer, my in-laws and brother-in-law accompanied my husband and me to the mall to shop for our upcoming vacation. There's a running joke that my husband isn't allowed to talk to people when we go anywhere because he quickly befriends them and ends up talking for three hours while the rest of us sit on a crowded bench. He's approachable and loves talking to people, so when he was stopped by a stranger while holding Nicholas, none of us were surprised. We all exchanged looks that silently said, *Uh-oh, here he goes again. We'd better catch up so we can stop him in his tracks.* I pushed the stroller filled with summer baby gear and more sunscreen than we would ever need a little faster.

As soon as I'd gotten within earshot of the conversation, I heard the man say, "I knew as soon as I looked at him that he was a Downs baby."

Now, I still didn't feel like the proper advocate that I am today, but I knew that "Downs baby" was the wrong way to refer to my son. Down was a person, and Nicholas is certainly not Down's baby. It's preferable to use "people first" identification. Nicholas was not a "Down syndrome baby," but a baby *with* Down syndrome. The fact that he was a baby came first. This way, the disability doesn't define the person in question. At that point, he had my attention.

"One of my sons is an autistic," he said as he gestured to one of the two teenage boys behind him. His thick Southern accent told me he wasn't from around here. I lowered my defenses for a moment, because not only was he a fellow special needs parent but referred to his own child without using people-first language. His son, who was a boy *with* autism and not "an autistic," looked a little embarrassed.

I thought, *Okay, this guy means well. I'm going to let him soak in another minute of Nicholas's cuteness and then we're out of here.* Sadly, Nick is way better at starting conversations than he is at ending them.

"I know that Downs people only live to be about forty-two, or even in their thirties, but I'll tell you there is an older Downs man I always see at McDonald's, and I always say, 'hello, how are you?' and he always says, 'I'm good, how about you?' and he's just the nicest guy. He's always happy and having a great time."

Hold on. Had this guy just given my child an expiration date? Could you imagine walking up to a family with a baby and estimating their baby's life expectancy? Could you imagine if my son was of an understanding age, and he heard someone say that he'll only live to be forty-two?

There are many factors that unfairly influence the life expectancy statistics for people with Down syndrome. People with Down syndrome, as you know, can be born with a variety of health complications, some of which are life-threatening. Also, the quality of care for people with Down syndrome has only just started improving within the last two decades. There are still some states today that don't allow people with Down syndrome to be on the receiving list for an organ transplant. So, although the statistics say that there's a lower life expectancy for people with Down syndrome, it's unfairly influenced by many different factors. It's also, I should mention, way older than forty-two.

His information was *extremely* inaccurate and outdated, but I didn't even know how to begin correcting him. In the moment, it didn't feel worth my time or effort. I was frustrated, I was taken off guard, and I just wasn't ready. My autopilot polite face was fading, and I was ready to leave. Even though I knew he just didn't have the right information, him telling us that my son would have a short life made me want nothing more to do with the conversation.

On the ride home, we all discussed what had happened. I felt bad afterward for being mad and rushing off. Ever since I became a teacher, especially since doing all this research on trauma-informed classrooms, I've seen the adults around me in a different light. To me, everyone I meet is a child carrying some sort of trauma. Even the people in my life I see regularly, I'll relate the research to them and wonder what baggage they're carrying around on a day-to-day basis and how it informs their actions. I think about what the major struggles of their life might've been, if I don't already know them, and wonder how it's shaped them into who they are as adults.

As mad as I wanted to be at this guy, my heart hurt for him. He wanted to connect with us about being a fellow parent of a special needs child, but he just didn't have the preparation, education, or social appropriateness to do so. I wonder if he was even a part of any support groups, or if he was all alone in this like we once were. This guy truly meant well, even if I didn't react well. He might not be in a situation where he can completely immerse himself in special needs education and advocacy like I can. He might not have the resources to learn as much as he can about his own child's diagnosis. I could also tell that he immediately regretted saying the life span thing once he saw my face.

Although I wanted to tell him it wasn't nice to tell a new mother her child will have a short life or that his information is incorrect, I'm glad I didn't. It's a shame he left us believing the same "facts" about Down syndrome that he came with, but I would've hated for our interaction to discourage him from reaching out to connect with other parents in the future. I know firsthand that connecting with other parents is a total life-changer even though it's scary at first.

Not everyone is as lucky as us.

The only reason I have all of this information on hand about Down syndrome is because I have someone extremely special in my life with Down syndrome. Not everyone gets to hang out with someone as amazing as Nicholas on a regular basis.

It wasn't the Down syndrome diagnosis alone that threw us for a loop in the beginning. It was the diagnosis paired with all of the false information that we had in our minds about Down syndrome. So, if I was so painfully uninformed, how can I assume everyone I meet to be scholars in developmental disabilities? It took me a long time and quite a bit of effort to be as informed as I am now. If it weren't for Nicholas, I would've gone on about my life not knowing these things. How can I be frustrated at people who aren't fortunate enough to have a reason to research Down syndrome? The best that I can do is kindly dispel misinformation I hear and make sure the people who approach me don't feel shut down.

The connection is the point.

Both the woman at Walmart and the man at the mall meant to do the same thing: connect. They saw us, saw something in common with us, and wanted to let us know about that in their own way. Neither meant to offend us or upset us. Shared experiences have the power to bring people together, and even though I felt bothered at the time, I had to look at the bigger picture. I want my kids to grow up seeing that even when I get frustrated, I try to understand where people are coming from.

Nicholas, as easygoing as he is, doesn't cry often. However, there's one thing that makes him cry every single time without fail, and that's seeing other people cry. If Marley's crying, he'll look along for a while as tears build up in his bottom eyelid. If we aren't able to calm her in time, he finds himself just as upset as she is. Nicholas, who people think will struggle to understand certain things, understands the most important thing of all: empathy. He sees someone crying and feels their pain so deeply he does the same. He's so naturally empathetic where a lot of people have to be taught how to be.

He reminds me to have empathy for others every single day, and I take that with me into every conversation I have.

Lesson 11

My son is more like other kids than he is different.

I realized this more as Nicholas got older and started to come into his own. But when he was a baby, it was brought to my attention in a very unique way. I could've read all the books, blogs, and websites in the world, but the most important lessons I learn in life are usually taught to me by the students in my classroom.

After five months of what I thought was going to be six-week maternity leave, I still wasn't ready to discuss my son's diagnosis with other people. I dreaded having awkward conversations with coworkers and pretending I was okay with it while enduring their involuntary condolence faces. I had no extra energy to devote to putting up a fake front for the adults, knowing I would already have to do that for my students. Just the thought of it sounded exhausting.

I was close to emailing the entire staff before I came back explaining my long absence and asking them not to discuss it with me. That's an odd impulse from someone so afraid of being isolated, but the fear made me irrational. I doubt anyone would even wave in the hallway after getting an email like that. My heart was tense and blocked up like I had to be ready to defend my son at any minute. It may sound extreme, but I was desperate to at least have my job be recognizable when everything else in my world wasn't.

Kids with Down syndrome have many things in common with their typical peers.

When my return date neared, I scoured Amazon for children's books about Down syndrome so that I could teach my class about it. I didn't even want to, but it was the beginning of March and I couldn't let my first World Down Syndrome Day come and go with no mention of my son at all. I wasn't ashamed of him; I was avoiding conversations I didn't know how to have. I had yet to have those conversations in my personal life, so I was completely out of practice.

It was slim pickings when it came to books, but I ordered two I thought were appropriate enough and also prepared a slideshow with some basic facts and pictures of Nicholas. As I was preparing these materials, I thought, *Wow, this is totally going to bore these kids.* They'd had a sub for the entire first half of the year since Nicholas was born on the first day of school, and she was a tough act to follow. However, when the day came to teach it, I was shocked at how engaged they were. We had no choice but to continue our conversation longer than I'd planned so that I could get to their endless stream of questions.

I explained that you can't "catch" Down syndrome and that it's not a disease; it just means you're born a little different. I told them it takes people with Down syndrome a bit longer to do certain things like learning to walk, run, ride a bike, or read. I gave my Lego analogy, which seemed to click with some of my future architects. Then, a student who rarely ever spoke up in class said something that changed my life right then on the spot.

"I have Down syndrome."

My defensive instincts kicked in as my heart started to race, though I kept a calm demeanor. *Is this kid going to try to make fun of my son already? Is the bullying starting this early?* I'd only known this student for a couple of weeks and knew very little about him. He was a struggling reader, and other teachers who didn't share my teaching philosophies called him a "behavior student," which only meant they struggled to make a solid connection with him. Even so, he and I had already become friends at that time, and I gave him the benefit of the doubt because he looked at me through his long curly hair with such concern and sincerity. His blue eyes didn't show even a hint of malice, so I kept the conversation going.

"Well, bud, you don't have Down syndrome. If you did, you'd already know it. Also, you would have some of the physical clues I just showed you."

"Well, I don't know, Mrs. Goo-Eye." This particular friend had trouble with my last name. "Everyone in this class can read except for me, and everyone on my street can ride a bike except for me. I say stuff wrong all the time. So, I think I probably have Down syndrome. I'll have to ask my grandma."

This student, who never participated in whole-group lessons before this, finally found a character in a story he related to--the character with Down syndrome who couldn't quite do the things all of her friends could. This boy related to my son without ever meeting him. Without knowing it, this child explained my situation to me instead of the other way around.

He taught me that my son *will* have things in common with his classmates. He *will* have people who share his struggles, frustrations, joys, and interests. Feeling behind because your peers can do things you can't do yet is an experience shared by millions of kids every single day, not just kids with Down syndrome. Nicholas doesn't have to be someone who only finds joy at home because the world outside doesn't understand him. My student already did. Maybe Nicholas wouldn't have to feel isolated after all. It was all I could do to not cry in the read-aloud chair.

After the lesson, I thanked that student over and over again. He thought it was because he finally participated in our class discussion. In reality, I thanked him for allowing my heart to relax and let other people in. I realized that conversations about Nicholas could help me instead of hurt me. Maybe talking to people about Nicholas wouldn't be so bad, because here I was doing it for the first time in my classroom and feeling a weight lifting off my shoulders.

I soon got excited about bringing my son around our friends more. They were all having children around the same time, and we were all experiencing the baby stage together. The collective children in the group have all spent the last few years growing from babies to toddlers together. None of them know Nicholas has Down syndrome, not because we don't want to tell them but because they simply don't care. They like to play with Nicholas the way he is, and even if things arise in life that pull them apart, they'll always love one another. To them, Nicholas is not a kid with Down syndrome. He's just their friend and playmate. When they're old enough to understand, telling them won't change their feelings about him.

Focus on the similarities.

Since that fateful day in my classroom, my World Down Syndrome Day school activities have gotten a lot more fun. I pair up with my teammate's class and ask the students to partner up with someone they know the absolute least about. Since we're working with another class, they're not as shy about this since many of them don't know the other kids well at all. Once we have our partnerships, we ask the students to interview each other, giving them examples of questions they can ask. *How old are you? How many siblings do you have? What do you like to eat? What do you do for fun?* While they're doing that, they organize the answers on a chart. One side of the chart shows the answers they had in common, and the other side shows the answers that made them different. I've done this for a few years now, and every time without fail, the partnerships have more things in common than they have differences. It sends the message to the kids that even though they might look different, they have so many more things about them that are the same. I love this activity because not only does it show them that people with Down syndrome are more alike than different, but it allows students to understand that getting to know someone personally can change the opinions of them that they might've had initially. I'll always teach my children and students to focus on the ways they relate to other people, instead of how they differ. This way they'll be more open to valuable connections and less susceptible to irrational judgments.

These students are growing up in a world where people fear differences instead of embracing them as beautiful and unique. They're witnessing the Black Lives Matter movement, the fear response of people crossing the border who simply seek asylum, and the cyberbullying that happens every single day. If nothing else, I want to teach my students not to fear differences, because our differences are what make us special. Maybe someday, they'll have a hand in reversing the unnecessary hate we see in our country. Maybe someday, they'll meet someone with Down syndrome and have the knowledge they need to greet them with the kindness and respect that he or she deserves, without fear.

The thought of people not accepting the person you love the most on this planet is heart-wrenching, but for every person who doesn't accept him, there will be fifty who love him unconditionally. My child is going to have more in common with his peers than differences, and I'm going to make sure he grows up knowing that fact.

Lesson 12

Parents need other parents.

It can be a very isolating feeling to deal with something without anyone to relate to what you're going through. At first, I didn't want to talk to any other parents of children with Down syndrome. I wouldn't have even known how to go about it or what to say because I didn't feel like a part of their club yet. How could I connect with other special needs parents when I hadn't yet dealt with special needs issues other than the diagnosis? I hated the thought of being a rookie and attempting to mingle with parents already in the big leagues. The last people I wanted to share my current state of identity crisis with were strangers. I decided to just figure out how I was going to manage this on my own, and that was the end of it.

Well, that didn't mean I stopped creeping on those families I found online through those magical hashtags. Their online presence made them seem a lot less scary, and their everyday routines seemed a lot like ours. Even though they all seemed famous with cute, catchy Instagram names, I realized that all of them started out just like me. Once in a while, I'd notice that some of them would travel long distances so their children could hang out with other kids their age with Down syndrome. I so badly wanted Nicholas to have friends who would be able to understand and relate to him on a level I couldn't. I needed to find a way to collect contacts who would provide Nicholas with these extraordinary friends. That's when I considered putting our lives out there on a social media platform dedicated to Down syndrome awareness.

One day while dropping Nicholas off to be babysat by his grandparents, I found myself chit-chatting with them for a while as I usually do. I can't recall what we talked about exactly, but it was something about how we didn't want Nicholas to be *limited* by what other people thought about him. As I was driving home thinking about the conversation, "Limitless Nicholas" popped into my head. The rhythm and rhyme of that phrase seemed too good to be true. This was it! This was our ticket in. My foot pushed a little bit harder on the gas pedal until I got home. I ran inside, purchased the domain name, and claimed the Instagram tag. I wasn't even sure on that day if I wanted to go through with being so public about my personal life, but I had to at least keep that option open.

Now, I've always loved writing. My bachelor's degree is in creative writing and cinema studies. I've always found joy in writing creative nonfiction, but that was with the understanding that no one would ever read my work. Buying this domain name meant people could read my story very easily, and that my "character" might not always be the good guy. Maybe the process of writing down my feelings would be therapeutic, and I could view the price of the domain name as a huge savings compared to therapy.

When I wrote my first post, it spent days in the "draft" folder of my blogging platform. When I look back on that first post now as someone who's been running a blog for years, it seems silly to think it took me so long to write something so short. I stared at it for days, opening and closing the browser window hoping the voice inside telling me to publish would just shut up already. *Is this good enough? What will people think? Oh man, everyone I know is on Facebook. How are they going to react to this?*

After days of staring at that post and triple-checking every word in it, I hit the publish button. I shared the link to my social media accounts late at night and then went straight to bed, hoping I would forget to ever check it again in the morning. *If I'm lucky, I shared this late enough that it will have been buried deep on everyone's newsfeed by morning.*

The next morning, fighting the urge to delete all of my social media apps and pretend like the share never happened, I opened up my accounts. What I found was an outrageous number of notifications and messages. People were thanking me, actually *thanking* me, for sharing my story. No one seemed confused or told me I was overreacting. No one wrote any sort of judgment toward me or my son. It didn't matter that none of the people I was friends with on social media had children with Down syndrome. People with kids who'd suffered some sort of trauma in the hospital connected with the post in their own way. Reading the comments didn't make me feel sick, it made me feel great. One comment in particular inspired me to just keep writing.

"Oh my gosh! I didn't know that! That is so interesting! I can't wait to learn more!"

Learn more? Someone who, like the old me, didn't know much about Down syndrome wanted to learn more? While I read the comments, I looked down at my five-month-old sidekick who'd become a nursing pro, no nipple shield required. I silently promised, *Don't worry, dude. I'll make sure they all learn a little more.* I had found a way to provide others with the knowledge I'd lacked, and it brought me so much joy.

Another comment said, "Thank you for this. My other mom friends just don't get it." That's been a recurring comment on my blog ever since. Yes, raising a child with Down syndrome isn't entirely different than raising a child without, but there are some things specific to us that I can't vent to my other mom friends about. This is when I realized how much I truly needed other parents to relate to.

After that, my posts became regular. Every time I thought I had nothing more to write about, something would happen that I knew wouldn't have happened if I didn't have a child with Down syndrome. I would then immediately share it to my blog. Sometimes when I take a long break from the blog, my husband will ask me why. I'll tell him I feel like I've said everything I can, and don't know what else I could possibly share. He'll then immediately list off five things that have happened since my last post, reminding me that I may be forgetting the fact that some of our situations are specific to us. This always causes me to hop back on with a handful of new posts, which always leads to a handful of new connections.

The best thing about having the blog and social media handles was that I no longer had to go through the terrifying task of seeking anyone out. All I had to do was post some adorable pictures of my son, which wasn't hard, tell what has been happening in our lives, and let people come to me. I used the same hashtags I saw over and over again, and the community just started growing. WordPress, the program that hosts my blog, allows you to see statistics of who's reading the blog. At first, I only had readers from my hometown and the city I live in now. Then, a few more flags were added to the roster. Eventually, I had twenty-seven countries reading his story. I even needed to utilize a translation app to respond to some of the international comments. It was starting to look like finding buddies for Nicholas wouldn't be so hard.

Eventually, I joined some Facebook groups for people who have children with Down syndrome. I always assumed I'd be a silent participant, but I have the most fun in those groups. There are often families that join immediately after getting their diagnosis and are swarmed with congratulations from all of us, instead of condolences. I always see parents validating one another about those first feelings of shock and grief that happen in the beginning, which is always when I tend to pipe in. Others post about their child going through a "terrible two" stage, which makes me feel better about Nicholas bossing us around from time to time.

The support I see people giving each other on those pages makes me so happy. I love when I scroll those pages to see a family who has just received a diagnosis and immediately turned to the groups to find support. It was something I hadn't been brave enough to do, and I admire them a lot for that. Also, there's the bonus of seeing photos of adorable babies daily. I learned that we don't have to know each other personally to genuinely connect on a personal level. Now, I have a place to have immediate access to other parents when I feel uncertain about something that arises with Nicholas.

One winter month of Nicholas's third year, I received two messages through Nicholas's social media platform. One was from someone I'd met briefly in college who'd reached out to me because she'd had a baby with Down syndrome. The other was from someone I'd never met before who'd just learned she was expecting a baby with Down syndrome. The best thing about this extremely lucky month was that both of these beautiful babies would be growing up in my son's hometown! If I hadn't created this large online presence, both of those people would've never known I existed, and Nicholas would have missed out on this super cool guy gang. Also, I would've missed out on this unique sisterhood I'd been able to form with the two mothers. I'm so grateful I took that life-changing plunge.

Don't just stare, share.

Even though our children are more alike than different, there are days when those differences feel concrete. As my son geared up for preschool the thought of this big change caused me a lot of anxiety. When I asked my friends about how they transitioned their child into preschool without them feeling scared or crying at drop-off, I got a lot of advice around explaining and modeling what school is like so that he knows what to expect when he gets there. Other moms said they bought new backpacks and school clothes to get their kids excited to start school.

This was one of those times where I was a little jealous of how easy mothers of typically developing children can have it sometimes. They can explain things to their children and make sure they understand what they're talking about because the child can ask them as many questions as they want. For me, I could explain it to Nicholas until I was blue in the face, but I couldn't be *sure* he knew what I was talking about because he couldn't directly show me. This was one of many times that moms without a child with special needs just wouldn't get it.

I hopped into the Facebook group and wrote my big list of concerns for them all to see. I received so many awesome tips, tricks, and ways to prepare us both for this big transition. More importantly, I was able to read a bunch of stories of how other moms endured the experience. Sharing my experiences instead of being a silent participant in those groups has given me the courage to get through so many difficult situations since then.

Be ready for in-person interactions too.

Finding people online is one thing. Hashtags and niche groups make it easy for us to connect with people with similar interests. Approaching people in person is an entirely different challenge.

One day, we were out Christmas shopping when we saw a young couple with a tiny baby. Since we couldn't help but walk by a little closer to see the little cutie, we noticed that she had some of the physical markers of Down syndrome. Our eyes lit up. Are these *our* people? Are these our new best friends? Not if they have no idea we're in their club, they're not.

Unfortunately, we didn't have Nicholas with us, so we couldn't exactly parade him around in front of them hoping they'd talk to us. We also noticed they seemed to be struggling a little to feed her, and we didn't want to overwhelm them further. We've had enough encounters with strangers in the mall to know it probably isn't a good idea to do it to someone else. We walked by them a couple of times as we tried to think of something to say, but eventually, we chickened out.

As we walked away, sad we didn't approach them, we talked about how we wished there was a way to tell them we're on their team without actually approaching and making them feel uncomfortable. We'd hated when the guy pointed out Nicholas's Down syndrome from across the mall, but strangely found ourselves in his shoes a few months later starving to connect with the other parents. Then, Nick came up with it, the idea that has us prepared for the next time this happens.

Business cards!

I know, it seems weird. We're not exactly selling anything and walking up to people and handing them a card is awkward. But since then, we've been able to approach people in a way that allows them to not talk to us at all in the moment but give *them* the choice to either reach out or not. They don't have to bear a conversation they find uncomfortable out of sheer politeness. They can see our website on the card, maybe read a post or two, and reach out if they want knowing we're local members of the Down syndrome team. We've also given some to our nurse friends, and when they meet someone getting a diagnosis of any kind, we can be there for them if they need us to be. Or, if they want, they can look us up on social media to assure themselves their lives are about to get exciting. My husband also gives them out at work when he's lucky enough to have a fellow Down syndrome parent in his barber chair.

Use the tools in front of you.

Another way to connect with families is by asking your therapists or service coordinator to help you make connections. They can't share information from other families for privacy reasons, but they can ask them if they're open to it. This is how we met one of the first families we connected with! Nicholas has had a couple of playdates with his buddy, who he shared some early intervention therapists with. I want Nicholas to grow up around people with Down syndrome. I want him to know he isn't always going to be "that one kid" in the group. Thankfully, because of social media and my blog, I've been able to make so many connections that I can soon use to Nicholas's advantage.

Sometimes, I take long breaks from the never-ending job that is advocating. Honestly, there are many times I forget that Nicholas even has Down syndrome because to me, he's just my son. But every once in a while, the parents in my groups will bring things to my attention that give me the tools I need to help Nicholas's development. They also share their stories so I can learn from their experiences, which is valuable in and of itself. A network of mothers and fathers can be a powerful thing. Even though my original goal was to find Nicholas people to relate to, I ended up finding the same thing for myself. We can't heal without a community, and I will forever be grateful that I found the courage to seek those communities out. I've become so passionate about bringing families together since I started my blog, and it's an honor that I wouldn't have had if I didn't have Nicholas. He has truly given me everything.

Doing
The Work

Once I connected with other parents, I finally had people to turn to when it came to all of the extra work behind the scenes that goes into raising a child with Down syndrome. People with Down syndrome tend to require a lot more practice when it comes to achieving their developmental milestones. That's why Early Intervention services exist. Early Intervention is the rolling out of speech therapy, occupational therapy, physical therapy, and/or special education to children between birth and preschool age who are falling behind in some way. This could be for kids with or without a diagnosis as long as they're considered behind in their development. Down syndrome is an "automatic qualifier" for these services in most states, since being behind developmentally is part of the diagnosis.

The idea behind Early Intervention, or EI, is to level the playing field as much as possible before the child enters the school system by having professionals come in to assist the families. Even with the help of professionals, success with developmental milestones has everything to do with the work you put into it when the therapists are *not* in your home. A therapist coming for a half hour once a week to work with your child is simply not enough to guarantee success. The point of their visit is to both work with your child while simultaneously showing you, the caregiver, how to better support their development.

Although I was so happy to start therapies with Nicholas, it wasn't easy. I suddenly had five appointments a week that I never had to juggle into my schedule before, and the day-to-day grind of it can be overwhelming. I had to learn new lingo, learn the strategies the therapists were teaching me, and make sure Nicholas was happy and ready to work hard. At the end of the school day, I used to look at the clock and feel a small sense of relief. During EI, however, I would look at the clock and think *okay, time to move fast.* From the school parking lot, I'd have to get into my car and hurry to Nicholas's babysitter's house, then race home to make his therapy session on time. Once therapy started, I had to stop and focus on the session while my mind still reeled from the day. Canceling would've been way easier, and I was tempted to do so many times. The magical thing about those sessions, though, was realizing that Nicholas could do way more than I would've discovered on my own. This was especially true because he was my first child, and I wasn't sure what kids his age were supposed to achieve in the first place!

One therapy session left me feeling upset with myself afterward. Nicholas was so small and was working on activating his core to reach for items held out of reach. The therapist had a toy in her hand that looked like it was miles away from him and expected him to reach for it. She might as well have asked him to reach up and grab a star out of the sky.

Good lord, he can't reach that, I thought as I watched and waited for her to inevitably give up on that task. I, of course, assumed that I knew every single thing my child was capable of doing. I was the one with him all the time, so wouldn't I know? He stared at those two plastic linking chains like they were hidden treasure, reached out his cute, chubby hand, gave a little "oomph," and snatched that thing out of her hand like it was no big deal.

"Wow!" I said, genuinely impressed. He surprised me so much that I laughed out loud. Immediately following my cackle, I felt a little guilty. I did what I'd been telling everyone not to do. I limited my own son's level of achievement based on what *I* thought he was capable of, without considering what *he* thought he was capable of. I would've never seen him reach for something so high if it weren't for that therapy session. I certainly wouldn't have thought to try the exercise myself. I was limited by my own imagination, just like the people whose minds I'm trying to change.

There have also been instances since then where the therapists would ask me if Nicholas could do something, and I would confidently say, "Oh yes, definitely" only to find that he wasn't able to do it. It was easy to imagine him doing something that seemed simple enough to me, but I had to think about these things realistically and imagine whether or not I'd seen him succeed at a certain task more than just a few times to be able to say he could do it "most of the time."

The therapists pushed Nicholas in ways I probably wouldn't have. I was too busy treating him delicately and not pushing him to try things on his own. I've seen him accomplish so many things I assumed he couldn't do during Early Intervention, and it has shown me that nothing is impossible for him as long as we're willing to put in the work.

What was really valuable during the sessions was the knowledge that *I* gained, not just what Nicholas learned. During the sessions, I witnessed so many different interventions I was able to easily add to our daily routines. I learned through these sessions that I had all the tools to make Nicholas successful in my house already, without having to pay a fortune for toys meant for children with developmental disabilities. I learned how to take the toys and household items we already owned and reimagine them to Nicholas's benefit.

One Christmas morning, while my kids were being spoiled beyond belief, I had recurring thoughts as Nicholas opened his presents.

Oh cool, we use something just like that in therapy.

Awesome, he can use that next time he has PT.

Oh, his therapist is going to love that one. She has a toy just like that.

It was that morning that I realized how truly anything can be a therapy toy as long as you use it properly. By using it properly, I mean using it with the background knowledge of how toys can be used as learning materials. For example, some people might look at a wooden knob puzzle with farm animals on it as just something to keep their child occupied for some time. When I look at that same puzzle, I see a way to work on hand-eye coordination, animal sounds, animal identification, directional work such as first, next, then, etc. There are endless possibilities as long as you're willing to work hard and educate yourself. The following section outlines lessons about how I both made the most of the professional help that was offered and incorporated things into my daily routines that benefitted my son's development.

Lesson 13

Early intervention isn't only for the child.

In those early days when I didn't want to talk to people, I was suddenly introduced to many thanks to early intervention. When Nicholas was enrolled in EI, I found us booked up with appointments with initial evaluators, service coordinators, and service providers. People I'd never met before had turned into weekly guests. At first, I saw them as outsiders who'd pop in every other day to remind me that my child needs extra support. However, once I started seeing the concrete value that came from the sessions, all of that changed.

When he started, he was five months old but seemed more like a two-month-old. When his first physical therapy session neared, I thought, *What on Earth is a physical therapist going to do with such a small baby?* I knew what physical therapy looked like from friends and TV and wondered how my little guy could possibly partake in such exercises. When she walked in, I handed my angel to her, and thus began my fascination with early childhood development.

After his initial evaluation, a goal was set for him to be able to make a fist. When I heard this, I thought about all the pictures I've seen of newborn babies in the hospital. They're screaming and making fists as soon as they're born. I wondered how she'd get him to do it as a five-month-old when it came naturally to other babies. She gently laid him on the ground and started working. She studied how Nicholas reacted to her physical cues, and then did many different exercises that caused him to react to those cues in the "correct" way. He used muscles I had never seen him attempt to use before, and I was fascinated. When she left, I couldn't believe how much there was to learn about how a child develops, and from then on looked forward to learning more.

I was more optimistic about his upcoming therapies after that. The next session on the menu was speech. Speech? Like talking? My baby was five months old, and I wasn't sure why we were signed up for speech. Again, my assumptions were dead wrong. Sitting Nicholas in his high chair, the therapist used tools in his mouth to train his tongue to do things like push food to his back molars and activate certain muscles in the mouth. She used strategies to get him to pop his lips and bring his tongue forward and back. I remember being thankful to have had Nicholas during a time in history where it's possible to intervene on childhood development at such an early age, because yet again he was doing things in that session I'd never seen him do.

As my level of excitement increased, so did my comfort level with the therapists. I was able to make my awkward jokes as I'd done in the nurse's station and found I had a few things in common with our weekly visitors. The sessions had gone from an uncomfortable social situation that made me nervous to a welcomed adult conversation that I was seriously deprived of. They began to add value to our lives beyond Nicholas's need for developmental assistance. Even though the visits became more comfortable, I still kept the visitors at arm's length for a time. That made it easier for me to blame them when things went bad.

Not every session was a miraculous "aha" moment. If sessions went badly, as they sometimes did, I used to view it as "their problem" and something I had no control over. Sometimes, a session would tank, and if paired with a long developmental plateau, I'd regret not canceling when I had the chance. The frustration would make me wonder if all of this extra stress was worth it if he wasn't going to make gains.

During one physical therapy session, Nicholas was extremely cranky. Physical therapy was the hardest and most exhausting since he had to exert the most energy. If he wasn't in the mood, he'd certainly not be shy about letting us know. At the time, he was learning how to walk, but things had been moving super slowly, and I think my impatience spilled over to him. The therapist and I tried to encourage him to try his best, but we only incited more grunts and stomps from him. In his anger, he grabbed the baby shark toy we were attempting to use as a motivator and stormed it over to me, stringing his stomps together with one long growl. She and I both jumped up and down and clapped, abruptly interrupting his mini tantrum. Without knowing it, Nicholas had just successfully walked while holding a toy instead of needing his arms up for balance for the very first time in his life.

I reflect on that particular session whenever I need to remind myself to be patient. When it comes to development, patience is the name of the game. His speech and physical therapists have both told me it's common for kids to make gains in one area while they sort of plateau in others. In the weeks before and after that baby shark session, Nicholas had made a lot of gains in speech and felt successful learning new signs and trying new sounds. So, even though he did accomplish something that day, his having to work super hard to be successful was the source of his frustration, which

I could understand since it was commonly the source of mine. I love that EI laid the groundwork for Nicholas to where he knows he'll have to work harder to learn things even when he doesn't feel like it. Celebrating that success with the physical therapist while also laughing at his temper tantrum was one of many times she showed me she wasn't just punching the clock. She was genuinely rooting for his success.

Therapists are members of the team.

They should be treated as such! All teams work better when they work as a unit. Members of the team need to be comfortable with each other in order to work well together. Each and every therapist who received Nicholas onto their caseload acted as not only a teacher but a cheerleader for him. It was me who was reserved in the beginning. I didn't have the knowledge to even brainstorm problem-solving ideas with them. Once I became more comfortable, I strived to create the kinds of relationships that allowed me to feel comfortable picking their brains and spit-balling ideas of my own.

Becoming close with our son's therapists also allowed *them* to feel comfortable telling us that certain products we bought might not be right for Nicholas, or that certain ways he sat might not be good for his muscle development. If you were doing something that was hindering the development of your child, wouldn't you want the therapist to feel comfortable enough to bring it to your attention? Allowing this kind of relationship not only helped Nicholas's progress, but gave me some new lifelong friends.

Pay attention and find opportunities to participate.

Every time there was a session, I'd take my regular place on the loveseat and watch. I didn't want to get in the way and wanted to allow the therapists enough space to do their work. Sometimes I'd watch while answering some emails on my phone. Other times, I'd be on Amazon buying whatever toy they were using with Nicholas while also eyeing the huge stack of clean laundry aching to be folded. *Would it be so bad if I left the room and just loaded the dishwasher?*

Although I was present for every session, I had to fight the urge to treat them as a parenting break. Early Intervention isn't just a half-hour session of work for the child. It's a learning opportunity for the caregivers. Although it's a nice workout for the child, the true purpose of the sessions is to allow parents to learn effective strategies they can implement to best support their child's development. For example, I learned that it prompts core strength to hold your child's hips when they're learning to balance on two feet instead of their hands, and that holding their hands can sometimes hinder their progress with balance. I wouldn't have learned it if I were in the other room eating a sandwich or putting the dishes away. During sessions, I could see how they worked with Nicholas while learning why those methods worked. I had opportunities to ask questions and try those methods with Nicholas in front of them to make sure I was doing it correctly.

Another way to participate in the success of the therapies are to make sure they're scheduled strategically. I used to schedule the sessions at times that I thought were best for *me*. When would *I* be dressed and ready? When would *I* be most focused? What time of day allows me to quickly tidy the house so that the therapist thinks it's always that clean? I later found the key to a great session was to schedule them at times that were best for Nicholas. Right before his nap or before a meal were bad times. He'd be hungry, tired, cranky, and mad at me for messing up his schedule. The last thing he wanted to do during those times of day was work hard. Instead, I'd schedule the sessions right after a nap or a snack. I made sure his basic needs were met so that he could put all his focus into what the therapists were teaching him and be way more willing to participate.

Creating a successful environment for the sessions made a huge difference. Instead of having them walk in on whatever we were already doing, I'd fix a space in the living room and gather any materials I thought we needed. Therapists usually bring their own toys, but if Nicholas achieved something I'd hoped to show them, I'd have anything we needed for that ready to go. I also took the ten minutes before therapy to "talk up" the session with Nicholas.

"Your friend is coming over, aren't you so excited?" I would ask while getting his favorite toys out. Then, when she would finally arrive, he'd be thrilled. That way, it wasn't something unexpected he had to mentally switch gears for, and it took a lot less time for us to convince him to participate.

His team appreciated the extra work I'd put in to ensure a successful session because it allowed them to get more effort out of Nicholas. The only downside was how sad Nicholas would get when they left! Trust me, we've had our fair share of sessions where Nicholas lay down on the floor in a peaceful protest and refused to work, but that was how we were able to figure out what worked for him and what didn't.

Do the homework and be honest when you don't.

After each session, it was common practice for the therapists would give us homework. At the beginning of EI, which lined up with my return to work, there were many weeks where I didn't remember or care enough to do the homework. When I was directly asked if we'd done it, I would say, "Yes, definitely" with a face that probably looked the same as the one I used when I lied about my homework in college.

After years of collaborating with therapists, I learned that knowing whether or not we truly did the homework can sometimes change the way they plan their lessons and future activities. For example, if we were asked to work on picking small objects up with his thumb and forefinger, and say that we worked on this every night, Nicholas's struggle to do this in the following session might cause unnecessary alarm for his occupational therapist. If she was under the impression that he'd worked hard on that skill for an entire week with the little outcome, she might be a little more worried about his progress. Therapists are better able to understand a child's development when they have an honest idea about what that child does every day.

In execution, it was hard to get into a routine where we were regularly doing the homework, especially when there were four different therapists giving us four different exercises to do. I had to learn to bite the bullet and be honest when we hadn't had the chance to do the homework. It always gave me a pang of mom guilt, but at least his team had an accurate picture of what Nicholas was achieving. After all, they only spent a half hour a week with him and needed all the information they could get.

Eventually, I learned how to weave Nicholas's homework into our daily routines so that it didn't seem so overwhelming. We now fold these practice skills into our daily lives in five-minute increments. If we can spend five minutes every night brushing his teeth, then we can regularly dedicate the five minutes prior to something else. Almost every homework assignment was disguised as a game, and Nicholas loved the extra attention he would get because to him, he was having fun with his mom. Instead of walking down the stairs, we counted each stair so he could practice saying and remembering his numbers. Little mindless changes like that have given Nicholas more opportunities to practice his skills throughout the day in a way that isn't time-consuming or exhausting for us.

Your baby can't be summed up in one evaluation.
Early intervention begins with the evaluation process. Before we were assigned therapists, we had some visit the house and evaluate Nicholas's existing level of development. After that, he was reevaluated every six months to check for growth. Although these evaluations often ended in my child getting more support or benefits based on his development, they also came with a mixed bag of emotions. On one hand, I got to see how far he'd come since the last evaluation. On the other, I had to listen to a bunch of people point out all of the things he couldn't do yet. This was especially painful when he wasn't yet walking but truly wanted to be. I longed to let him run around and play in the backyard or go explore places that he hadn't been able to before. It didn't feel fair that Nicholas couldn't do those things when he was working a lot harder at it than his peers. Now that he's walking all over the place and dancing his days away, all of his hard work in therapy was well worth it.

When it was time to transition out of early intervention and into preschool, Nicholas had to be evaluated again to give his new therapists at school a baseline to work with. I was thrilled with the progress he'd made to this point and was excited for this round of evaluations. He was walking, communicating his basic needs with sign language, and finding a new and fun playmate in his sister, who'd just started walking herself.

Since it was the middle of the coronavirus pandemic, these evaluations were done via video chat by people who weren't already on his team so that their comments could be completely impartial. Working with his existing team would've been tough through a screen, let alone complete strangers. Since they were realistic about the fact that a simple half-hour call wouldn't be able to tell them everything they needed to know, much of these evaluations were done based on parent interviews. Even so, we tried to show them as much of Nicholas as we could during that time.

The physical therapy evaluator asked if Nicholas could kick a ball. "Oh, yes, he loves soccer!" my husband and I reported excitedly. I turned the camera around to show that particular skill off. We put the ball in front of Nicholas and said, "Go ahead, buddy! Kick it!" He walked toward it with a big smile and "kicked" the ball like he always did.

"Oh, I see, he doesn't exactly kick the ball as much as he just walks into it," she said, dictating her notes out loud to us.

This triggered my defensive mommy brain. *Hey, lady! If he's having fun, he's doing it right! He can play soccer any way he wants to!* But the evaluator wasn't looking to see if Nicholas could have fun; she was looking to evaluate his developmental abilities. It was a good thing that she asked us to have him kick a ball in front of her instead of taking our word for it because we'd confidently told her he was a soccer superstar! We didn't know those kicks weren't exactly up to snuff.

I had to remember what I'd learned about the benefit of complete and total honesty when it came to evaluations. It would be a disservice to Nicholas to give inaccurate information to this person, even though my heart wants to always shout Nicholas's achievements from the rooftops. It's the job of the evaluating therapists to put some focus on the things your child can't *yet* do. Even though it stung to hear negatives when Nicholas had been working hard all summer, I had to have an open mind. I had to be honest with the situation at hand and make sure I was communicating clearly with the therapists and evaluators.

A few weeks later I received the official written evaluation from the therapists in the mail and read through the intimidatingly thick document. I read sentences like "he can kick a ball, but he is more walking into the ball than lifting his foot to swing it forward" and

"Nicholas's speech delays make it very hard for him to communicate at the level appropriate for his age." Of course, these people had only seen a snippet of who Nicholas is as a person, but one person hit the nail on the head when she wrote her summary. One of the lines I highlighted in her report said, "Nicholas is a good friend." You're damn right, lady. It's the thing he does best. I hung that page on the fridge, proud that Nicholas was able to show that to a stranger in a short video chat session. No report can properly capture all that is my son, and I'm sure to remember that every single time I receive one.

Celebrate every single achievement.

This works especially well for my son. Nicholas loves celebrating his successes, and the prospect of more accolades always drives him to try harder. As soon as he learned to clap, he realized that we use clapping in our world to show someone they've done a good job. Sometimes when he did an activity incorrectly, he'd clap and look at us. When he saw we weren't clapping, he knew he had to do something different. That allowed him to get immediate feedback on tasks he was doing without needing to have strong communicative skills. Then, an even bigger celebration was in store for him when he did it correctly.

Aside from providing immediate feedback for Nicholas, celebrating his achievements gave us time to reflect on how far he'd come. From simply asking him to make a fist to running in the backyard playing "red light, green light," the transformation was amazing. The journey was even more so.

By the end of the three years, my role in early intervention changed quite a bit. My spot on the loveseat would often be vacant. Instead, I'd be on the floor with the therapist and Nicholas acting as another set of hands in each exercise. Some days, he'd walk back and forth between the physical therapist and me, probably loving that two of his best friends were giving him so much attention while he strengthened his leg. Full participation, honesty, and communication played a huge role in Nicholas's success in the early intervention program.

Lesson 14

Communication is key.

Imagine being in a room with your family. Everyone's hanging out, chit-chatting, and having a nice time. Now, imagine you can understand everything that everyone says, but no one can understand you. Sounds frustrating, doesn't it? As Nicholas grew from a baby to a toddler, I began to see this frustration bubble up in him.

This frustrating time isn't specific to babies with Down syndrome. For all kids, there's a gap between the time they can identify their own basic needs, and when they're able to communicate those needs to their caretakers. They might feel hungry or thirsty, but the adults can't seem to get what they're trying to communicate no matter how much they grunt or stomp. Perhaps, those behaviors are viewed as the child "being a brat." Having gone through this with two kids, I've come to realize how important effective communication is when it comes to dampening the "terrible two" stage.

Hypotonia, or low muscle tone, is common among people with Down syndrome. It affects all the muscles in a person's body, including the muscles in the mouth. A common misconception is that people with Down syndrome are born with large tongues, which adds to their communication difficulties. The more likely source of the difficulties is small facial features being a physical marker of Down syndrome. A child could have a small mouth, nose, and eyes, but a typically sized tongue. This requires even more control of the mouth muscles to speak clearly. Because of this, people with Down syndrome have a wide range of communicative abilities from speaking clearly to being nonverbal, and anywhere in between.

This is why speech in early intervention is so important for babies. It allows therapists to train the muscles in the child's mouth in a way that prepares them to make many of the sounds in speech. As I watched them work with Nicholas every week, I prepared to endure a longer time period when Nicholas and I would struggle to communicate with each other.

Of course, after the initial diagnosis, I'd read online that "people with Down syndrome *will struggle* to communicate." That was it, plain and simple. Now that I know the range is so wide, I can't believe the author of that statement could even write something like that without knowing every single human on the planet with Down syndrome. Perhaps he or she meant to refer to the longer time period it could take for a child with Down syndrome to effectively communicate. Even so, I'm here to tell you that communication is not impossible.

Sign language is a lifesaver.

Thanks to the sign language I learned through Nicholas, he was able to communicate his basic needs to me long before he could talk. One day, when he was just a crawling baby, I turned the bathtub on and asked Nicholas if he wanted to take a bath. He absolutely loved bath time but was pouting and grunting when I brought it up. Confused, I went into the bathroom and waited for him, hoping he would follow me.

From the bathroom, I heard more grunting followed by the sounds of aggressive crawling. I assumed he was making his way to the bathroom, but he never arrived. When I went back out to look for him, I found him in the kitchen sitting next to the cupboard where we kept all the snack items. There he sat, looking me straight in the eyes, signing the word "eat."

I couldn't believe my eyes! It wasn't the first time he'd ever signed the word, but it was the first time he'd used it unprompted by me or a therapist. He was finally using it for what he needed. Of course, he didn't want to take a bath. He was hungry! He had the tools he knew he needed to tell me so, and he used them. That was the first time he was able to communicate his needs to me, and I was overjoyed. Since I wanted to show him that he'd done the right thing by telling me what he needed, he had way more snacks than he probably anticipated.

> > >

Years later, when Nicholas was halfway through preschool, my husband caught COVID-19 and had to quarantine downstairs while me and the kids quarantined upstairs. We didn't have COVID-19, but we did have sinus infections, and all three of us were miserably sick. After over a week of being cooped up in the house, I was ready to lose my mind. I needed to get out and knew the McDonald's drive-through in our town was extra safe. They stuck the credit card reader into your car window on a pole so there was no chance of contamination. So, I decided to use junk food to bribe my kids to eat, since their sickness had killed their appetites.

I walked up to Nicholas and asked, "Do you want to take a ride in the car?"

He responded by clapping and signing "shoes, help." After being stuck in the house for so long, I needed that moment. It was the first time I'd ever seen Nicholas use two signs consecutively to communicate a phrase. What he was probably trying to say was "finally, lady, help me with my shoes so we can get the heck out of here for a minute," but the two signs in a row were plenty for me to celebrate. Every once in a while, he shocks me with some new communicative skill, and it makes me so excited for the future.

The best part of sign language for Nicholas was that he didn't have to execute it perfectly to get his point across. Our therapists called this "sign language slang." For example, the sign for "water" is making the number three with your hand, which is the sign for the letter W, and raising it to your cheek. Nicholas signs water by placing the heel of his hand on the side of his chin with the rest of his fingers fanned out since he struggled with the fine-motor skills required to touch his thumb to his pinky. Marley signs "water" by placing her whole hand on her cheek and looking at me with intent. Neither of those signs are perfect signs for the word "water," but that really isn't important. The point is, I'm able to tell when my kids need a drink without their needing to verbally communicate that to me. We can work on perfecting those signs when they get older if they still need them. That way, more people than just me can understand them.

Even without having all of the signs or all of his letter sounds, Nicholas can react to language prompts in an appropriate enough way. Before he could say or sign "yes" and "no," he was able to show us those answers. "Yes" would look like smiling and clapping. "No" would be pouted lips and shaking a finger while his head tilted to one side. Some of his sign language is specific to him, like when he asks me to dance. His sign for "dance" is making two fists and putting them up to his chest. This is nowhere near the real sign for "dance," but we know what he means when he does this and are quick to turn the music on. Even though he isn't communicating with the "correct" tools, I want to make sure he knows he'll always be rewarded for trying to tell us his wants and needs.

Receptive language is a powerful thing.

Right around the time that Nicholas began communicating his needs to us, I had a student in my class with apraxia of speech. Apraxia of speech is a difficulty some people have when it comes to the motor planning needed to make certain speech sounds. Although it was difficult for my student to communicate verbally, I noticed something interesting. He could consistently get perfect scores on vocabulary tests, science tests, and any other assessment based on the information I gave orally. The guy, I learned, soaked in every single word I said even though he wasn't able to show me that verbally. There was absolutely no reason for speech difficulty to stop him from being successful in school. He had strong receptive language skills.

Receptive language is the ability to comprehend spoken words. I wondered if Nicholas could somehow start to show me he could understand what I was saying. Sure, he couldn't talk yet, but could he respond to verbal cues? That was when I started talking out loud all day long.

Everywhere I went in the house, everything I touched, everything I did was dictated out loud. Back then, my husband worked at a restaurant and was not home in the evenings. So, it was just Nicholas and me in what would've been a quiet house. But it wasn't quiet. I spent every night yammering on at every given opportunity. If it was time to put his shoes on, I would say something like "let's go get your shoes, Nicholas. We have to put them on your feet because we're leaving the house. We keep them in your room by your bed, so let's go get them. Okay, one foot at a time. One. Okay, other foot, please. Two! There we go! Now we're ready to leave!" My dogs stared at me like I was completely insane, but as time went on, I noticed a big change. Of course, I could've gotten the shoes myself, then plopped him onto my lap and put them on. That would've probably been a lot faster, but it would've also removed the learning opportunities involved with doing it the hard way. Now, I can casually ask Nicholas to go get his shoes out of his room for me and after only one direction he'll run and grab them, bring them back to me, and sit on my lap so I can help him put them on.

Not only does this strategy help Nicholas with his receptive language skills, but it also provides him with more exposure to the sounds of speech. The more he's exposed to those sounds and watches me make them with my mouth, the faster he'll learn to make them himself. Other than seeming like a lunatic to any visitors, it's a win-win!

Once Marley joined the family, I noticed that Nicholas wasn't the only one who benefitted from my endless chatting. Every time I wanted the kids to take on a new routine, I would spend a few weeks saying that routine out loud, and sometimes rhythmically. The winter where Nicholas was three and Marley one and a half, I started saying "shoes and coats" a lot when we walked through the door. After a couple weeks, they adopted the habit of sitting on the bottom steps when they got home from school and taking off their own shoes and coats before going upstairs. I can say, "Time to brush your teeth" or "Time to go to bed" and both children will head in the direction of those activities without a second thought. My consistent talking also allowed Marley to have more exposure to the sounds of speech, and she's always eager to practice with me even though Nicholas taught her all the signs he knows.

Our kids deserve the chit-chat they crave.

If you've ever spent any time with a toddler, you know that most of them love to talk. Even though Nicholas cannot yet talk the way his peers can, he's no exception. Every day when I pick him up from the babysitter, I ask him what he did at school. However, I don't ask him that exact question as it's too open-ended for him. I ask him about specific activities. "Did you play with blocks? Did you paint? Did your teacher read a book? Did you eat lunch?" After each question, Nicholas is able to answer me with a yes or no. Just because his language isn't as developed as mine doesn't mean he can't share his day with me.

It's always a little heart-wrenching to see Nicholas's typical friends talk to him expecting a response that Nicholas can't yet give them. It makes me afraid that in one fleeting moment he's lost the opportunity to connect with another kid. I would love to see him chatting back and forth with friends so that he doesn't feel left out and can't wait for that to happen. But, while I wait, the best I can do is work with him every day to make sure I'm giving him every opportunity to be successful in this area.

While we wait for Nicholas to hone his speech skills, I love teaching sign language to all the other kids in our lives. They love learning it and treat it like a secret language they share with Nicholas. I also let them use the flashcards or other visual cues I have to aid Nicholas's communication so they can participate in Nicholas's way of communication, instead of Nicholas always being expected to participate in theirs.

No doctor, therapist, or statistic will be able to predict how well *my* child will be able to communicate. The only thing I can do is make sure he has all of the tools he needs to have as much success as possible. From my experience, adding things to my daily routines such as talking out loud even when it seems unnecessary have helped Nicholas hone his receptive language skills and become an overall better communicator.

Lesson 15

Letting my son struggle only *feels* mean.

This was one of the hardest lessons for me to learn.

As a teacher, I can't spend math class simply teaching math. If I did that, I'd spend a lot of time spouting off math content to children who neither know nor care about what I'm saying. Before I get to teaching the actual math lessons, I first have to invest hours into teaching the children they're human beings who are capable of learning math. I need them to believe deep down that they're smart enough and good enough to learn new things. Without that, they'll never be invested enough in themselves to even try to do a math lesson with me. If I never address that step, my students might get through the entire school year never believing themselves worthy enough to have this new life skill.

I keep this idea in mind every day with Nicholas. Again, telling people your child has Down syndrome is hard because they tend to offer you sympathy at a time where you don't exactly want it. This act of being offered sympathy at first made me think I actually needed it, and that idea tricked me into thinking I *should* be feeling bad for myself and my son. *If everyone is offering me sympathy, that means I should pity him, right?*

As a result of this needless pity, I found myself over-helping Nicholas as he developed. When I first came to terms with the diagnosis, I worked so hard to convince other people that having a child with Down syndrome is like having a typically developing child, and in the most important ways, it truly is. However, when it comes down to the day-to-day practice of it all, there are times where it'd be easy for someone to hold their child back without meaning to simply because the world told them to feel bad for their child.

At first, it felt like being a special needs mom would never get easier. Jealousy of other mothers would sometimes rear its ugly head. I thought things like, *Wow, this is so unfair. Other kids would be able to walk themselves up the stairs without leaving their moms to take three trips inside from the car every single day after work.* His having Down syndrome existed in my mind as something that caused extra work for me because he *needed* me more than other kids need their parents. It's easy for me to see now how some parents fall into the routine of doing too much for their kids, special needs or otherwise.

Patience over pity.

I discovered that Down syndrome is no reason to feel sorry for someone. It's a reason to hone your practice of patience. I thought my patience improved once I became a teacher, but since Nicholas was born it has become my superpower. It'll take Nicholas longer to learn how to do things than it would a typical child, period. That's the reality he lives in, and I need to teach him to be successful in that reality. If I constantly help him with things because I'm impatient or feel bad for him, he might start to believe he's not smart enough or good enough to be able to learn them on his own. More so, I don't want my impatience to be the reason he develops those feelings deep down.

Just as asking Nicholas to get his shoes instead of me getting them is more time-consuming than me getting them myself. The point is not to be efficient. The point is to practice his life skills as often as possible. It's so important to me that he gains independence so that he can be successful on his own, without needing the help of anyone. If I'm unable to wait for Nicholas to show me what he knows, I won't be able to figure out what he doesn't know yet. That in itself makes it worth the wait.

So, I decided to switch the routine of coming home from school. I'd park the car in the driveway, run my bags inside, come back out, and take Nicholas out of his car seat at the bottom of the stairs instead of the top. He'd then slowly make his way to the top of the stairs on his own, grunting and sweating the whole way. Sometimes, he'd get halfway up, turn around, and look at me as if to say, *Aren't you going to help me at all, lady?* This would always give me a pang of mom guilt, but my belief at the time was that he has to work harder to learn his daily tasks, and the stairs were only an example of that. Just as he has to adjust to his reality, I have to do the same. Every single time, I feel like the meanest mom on the planet, but I know I'm doing what's right for Nicholas, no matter how exhausting these tasks seem to be for him.

Set the bar high.

According to research on educating children with Down syndrome, if a child with Down syndrome is taught by someone who has low expectations of them, they're likely to develop learned helplessness. This means the structure of their life has led them to believe they're not capable of completing certain tasks, so they don't even bother trying. For example, if a teacher's aide helps a child with a disability put their coat on and take their coat off every single day, that child might think they aren't capable of completing this task on their own and will always ask for help. This is not the life I want for Nicholas. Instead of thinking, *Well, he has Down syndrome, so he doesn't have the muscle tone or fine motor skills to put on his own coat*, I want them to think, *Well, he has Down syndrome, so I better give him as much practice as I can to put on his own coat since he has low muscle tone and fine motor difficulties.*

Let me be the first to admit that this step is *so* hard and sometimes maddening. There have been so many times I want to just do things for Nicholas so I can get them done faster. Walking him up the stairs took four seconds while letting him do it could take as long as ten minutes. Unzipping his coat for him would take a fraction of a second, but instead, I wait the painstaking few minutes for him to do it himself. I'm not the most patient person in the world, but more than I want things to be done fast, I want Nicholas to know he can do them himself.

At the time of writing this book, Nicholas is three years old, and I still lift him into the car seat. I've only just started the process of having him climb into the car himself so I can buckle him in. I know it'll be worth it because he needs to know how to do that himself, but when we're in the driveway running late in the freezing weather, the stress of waiting drives me crazy! He's getting heavy, though, and hoisting him up into the back seat of a van takes all of my strength. The more practice he gets doing this on his own, the sooner I can retire from my heavy toddler lifting gig.

Learning to do new tasks on his own is not the only benefit I see from being patient and allowing Nicholas to do his tasks independently. I also see a huge improvement in his overall perseverance. When he first started using silverware, he used to get frustrated right away when the little plastic baby fork wouldn't stab the food. He'd show us his frustration by chucking the fork across the room. Now, after many hours of practice, he'll sit with his fork in his hand for as long as it takes for him to stab the food so he can eat it, soaking up every bit of praise that comes his way as a result.

There was one time in particular at Marley's first birthday party when I cut up a cupcake for him and gave him a fork to eat it. I ended up recording the whole process since I was so impressed with what came next. As a lover of cake myself, I was fully expecting Nicholas to ditch his time-wasting fork and just go for it, especially since his sister was next to him going bananas on her smash cake. We even removed his shirt, hoping to save it for the mess we expected would happen. Instead, he sat there with his face full of concentration and took his time to get every single bite onto his fork and gently bring it to his mouth. Had he been wearing a shirt, it would've come away from the experience unscathed.

Perseverance is a very difficult skill to put into practice. The desire to give up because something is hard can be so tempting. Nicholas had arguably the most valuable thing for a toddler right in front of him: birthday cake. He still chose to take his time and eat it the way he'd been practicing so he could be proud of himself. I saw patience from a two-year-old that day that I don't see from some adults, and it was honestly impressive.

When people are at my house, I can often tell they're shocked when I ask Nicholas to clean up his own toys or ask him to retrieve something he threw down the stairs. As my stern expression meets his innocent one, he'll turn around and get right down to business. He has strong receptive language, and he can understand that something he did was wrong and that he has to fix it. Even so, I sense the shock while Nicholas starts picking up his blocks and putting them back into his toy chest. But Down syndrome or not, he's still a toddler. He doesn't get a pass because he can't communicate with me efficiently yet. He knows the deal, and I don't want him to think someone will just help him with his mess because he has Down syndrome. I'd hate for that sentiment to carry over into school and then eventually into adulthood.

Of all of the lessons in the book, this one makes me cringe the most. It's so hard for me to reel in the control I try to have of everything around me. But the bottom line is, I want Nicholas to be okay without me. I don't want him to need me to survive. I want him to need to talk to me every day and be my best friend, but if anything ever happened to me, I want him to be okay. That's why I put myself through this painstaking process of pushing independence. I hope his teachers and everyone else who works with him throughout the years do the same. In my opinion, it can only help him see his true potential. I want him to know the same thing I do—that he's capable of achieving whatever he wants as long as he's willing to put in the hours of hard work it may take to get there.

Lesson 16

Developmental deadlines are bullshit.

Kids should be eating solid foods by six months old. Kids should be walking by one, and definitely off the bottle by then too. My kid is going to be so behind. He'll never catch up with his peers.

Those thoughts used to run through my head daily. Looking back, I can't believe I ever worried about *when* my child would succeed. The timing of success when it comes to his development seems utterly meaningless to me now.

There are certain developmental deadlines that exist for babies. Of course, I understand why these imaginary deadlines exist. It's extremely helpful for typically developing children to have these deadlines so their parents and/or doctors can recognize whether or not they're in need of early intervention or any other medical support. But I still wish there was a wider acceptance of children who don't fit into those particular molds, or that these ideas were presented to parents of children with Down syndrome a little differently.

Most parents have this one thing in common: they think their children are the best children ever. Of course, they're all correct. There's no child like the one you created from scratch and brought into this world. Unfortunately, this level of love and admiration doesn't stop parents from comparing their children to other children whether the child has a disability or not. The habit of comparing people to other people can be toxic, and popularized developmental deadlines can act as fuel for those comparisons and cause unnecessary anxiety and feelings of inadequacy for both the parents and the children. Add the fact that children with Down syndrome are "destined" to be behind, according to research, and the pressure can be overwhelming. After receiving a Down syndrome diagnosis, it's easy to fear that your baby won't develop as they "should." You worry about what people will say, or how much extra work it'll be to get them to do basic things. What I should've been worrying about was what I was going to do to make sure he knows it's okay to succeed at your own pace.

This is a topic that comes up for me a lot, both in my personal life raising children and my professional life as a second-grade teacher. In one instance, I was about four days into teaching my students about a certain subtraction strategy, which is usually right around the time where the students start to decide that they don't like subtraction. Subtraction is always intimidating to kids, so I take it slow each year usually adding a few days to the suggested teaching time that our school's pacing guides allow. About halfway through one lesson, I heard a little whispered gasp followed by a girl's voice on the rug saying, "Oh my gosh, I get it now" as she scribbled her answer onto her whiteboard. Those small moments are what I love about teaching. Kids working hard to finally understand something hard for them at first.

Were there kids who understood what I was teaching on the first day I introduced it? Sure! Were there kids who still struggled with it? Absolutely. The point is, they're not required to understand it at the same moment. That one student was able to have their "aha!" moment that day, and I was as proud as I could be of that student's success. I wasn't dwelling on the fact that they didn't learn it the first time I introduced it, or that I still hadn't reached every student in the classroom yet. The best thing I could do for that one student was to give her all the tools she needed to succeed and guide her and her peers through some practice.

The same is true for developing babies. Just like in my math lesson, the best thing I can do for my children is give them all the tools they need to be successful and guide them through some practice. By enrolling Nicholas in early intervention, communicating with therapists about best practices, and using those methods regularly outside of sessions, that's exactly what I did. That's all we can do. Educate ourselves and practice, practice, practice!

> > >

It's hard being a mother of a child with special needs for countless reasons, but the perceptions of others is the biggest one for me. Everyone seems to have an opinion on what you're doing, and if you're doing it right. Commonly, parents of children with disabilities are either told that we're giving our children too much assistance or not enough, all based on what other people think of the child's level of abilities. Either way, we aren't doing the right thing according to the world because our children are viewed as imperfect, and therefore, so is our parenting.

The framework society has put in place for us doesn't help our situation in the least. There's such a mixed bag of beliefs and ideals when it comes to disabilities in general. Ideas range from people believing that people with different abilities should be valued or celebrated to others thinking those people should have never been born.

The problem isn't with Nicholas's extra chromosome. The problem is the way society has been trained to view what his "disability" means.

The problem isn't that he may have difficulty learning in school. It's that school is set up to only give a differentiated level of instruction to a few individuals, which makes the difference between some kids and their typical peers extremely noticeable.

The problem isn't that I have a child with Down syndrome. The problem is that people have been trained to see Down syndrome as an imperfection, as opposed to just another human trait.

It took me a long time to realize the negative ideas perpetuated by our society about children with Down syndrome don't have to impede our lives. The bottom line is that kids develop at different speeds, no matter how many chromosomes they have.

The child's timeline is the right timeline.

Walking is considered a major milestone, and one that all parents make sure to heavily document. "Is he walking yet?" was a question we got from almost anyone who asked us how old Nicholas was. Saying no was always a little heart-wrenching, especially because it tended to bring people's condolence faces back into view. Even worse, we sometimes received aggressively confused looks when we'd say no, implying that there was something deeply wrong with this. Whether the people knew he had Down Syndrome or not, this always made me uncomfortable.

To give us some motivation to work hard, we said Nicholas would walk by the time he had his second birthday. He'd been so close for so long, and we practiced every single day, but it just wasn't happening. His birthday came and went, and he still wasn't walking. In hindsight, I regret putting the pressure of walking by his second birthday on our family. Having completely invented expectations lead to unnecessary disappointments. Again, the problem wasn't that Nicholas hadn't walked by the age of two; the problem was that the world told me walking later than the age of one is a huge problem. So, walking after the age of two seemed to encourage twice the concern

In November of that year, two months after his second birthday, he started taking independent steps. Since it was something that we worked so long and so hard for, it was much more worth celebrating. We posted videos of him taking his steps as he held his little arms above his head for balance, and the outpouring of support was amazing. We received thousands of comments congratulating Nicholas for all of his hard work, and we were so happy to share our celebrations with the world. At that moment, it didn't seem to matter how long it had taken him to reach that milestone. The fact that he reached it was enough. It didn't matter when he was supposed to walk, when we said he would walk, or when other kids with Down syndrome started walking. The point was that he did it.

Comparison is pointless.

When Nicholas was learning sign language, it took a ton of work to get him to use it in context instead of simply because he was copying what we were doing. My husband and I would casually use it in context every single day so that he'd see how it was supposed to be used, and then hope he'd eventually pick it up. When you think about it, that's exactly how kids learn spoken language, so we wanted to give Nicholas every opportunity to learn both.

One day, while mindlessly scrolling social media, I came across a video of my friend's child, who was about nine months younger than Nicholas, using a variety of signs in the proper context. This child doesn't have a diagnosis; she just has a great mom who taught her early communicative skills as many moms do. Without even knowing that it would bother me, I started sobbing.

I couldn't even believe my reaction because I considered myself more patient than most when it came to development. I think my reaction to that video came from a place of feeling that my son wasn't getting a fair shot. I felt like it was unfair that after months of working hard with professionals, Nicholas still wasn't at the point of using his signs correctly. This child, on the other hand, could pick it right up because she had the privilege of not having any developmental delays. It was truly a hard moment because I wanted to be happy for my friend's daughter, but instead I had to sit on my living room floor and shed pointless tears, jealous that another child could have things easier than my son.

I was also thinking of his future baby sister, who I was pregnant with at the time. I didn't even know what she'd be like. I imagined her as a typically developing child, as we all probably do unless we receive a diagnosis during pregnancy. What would he think when her development surpassed his? Would that make him feel sad? What could I do to protect him from this? The truth is, we can't protect our children from every bad feeling we anticipate; we can only make sure they know they can come to us when they come up. So far, I've seen Nicholas be nothing but fully supportive of his sister, clapping his hands every time he sees her succeed at just about anything.

It has been common in my journey to have moments of disappointment that other kids can have things my son can't, achieving them much faster than my little hard worker. I have to actively remember not to compare my child with other children, or he'll grow up comparing himself to everyone else. It would kill me to think I gave Nicholas the tools to have doubt or be disappointment in himself. Instead, I hope to raise Nicholas to truly believe he is unique and special in his way. I want him to see himself in the same magical way I see him.

As far as Marley's development goes, just being our daughter and having Nicholas in our family is going to make her hardwired for patience, and she'll understand Nicholas more than anyone else can. I can also see by their interactions in the house every single day that being supportive of each other has come naturally to them, and I'm excited to see that blossom as they get older.

My friend, who taught her daughter sign language despite her not having a diagnosis, was in a way addressing one of the societal problems I laid out earlier. Nicholas has to learn sign language to bridge the gap between expressive and receptive language *because* he has Down syndrome. The problem isn't that his low muscle tone requires him to find another way to communicate. The problem is that our country generally accepts one form of communication: spoken American English. She's teaching her daughter sign language, which will eventually allow her daughter to communicate easily with my son. She's helping me build a world Nicholas can thrive in as opposed to one where no one understands what he's saying unless they have a reason to learn sign language.

It's not my child's fault that people expect certain things of him by a certain age, nor is it my fault for not working on development twenty-four hours a day. Instead of allowing those deadlines to make me upset, I think about what I can do to change people's perspective on development. There's a lot I can achieve in my lifetime when it comes to spreading awareness and making sure my child's world is filled with modes of accessibility. I can't help that Nicholas lives in a world where people will build up walls to stop him from succeeding, but I can grab my sledgehammer and help him knock them down.

Lesson 17

It's okay to have more kids.

I was nine days past my due date, so I had to be induced. I turned myself in for this one. There would be no spontaneous labor moment that forced me to buck up and get it done; just us waiting for the clock to strike seven a.m. As I walked into the hospital that morning, I had the same four thoughts I always have when I'm next in line for a roller coaster:

1. *I'm excited*
2. *I'm scared*
3. *What if I die?*
4. *Why the hell did I get in this line in the first place?*

Nick and I thought it would be fun to get up super early and go to a diner for sort of a "last meal" before the big show. Nicholas was with his grandparents, so we had some freedom to do what we wanted before reporting for duty. Since we were so excited, we were annoyingly early. We finished our breakfast with an hour to spare. Sitting at our local diner with the elderly breakfast crowd, we could tell by their smiles they knew where we were headed.

"Let's go visit Nicholas on the way!" my husband said as he paid the check.

For some reason, this sparked panic inside me I hoped would put me into labor the old-fashioned way. What was I doing here? How could I have done this?

What is going to happen to Nicholas?

> > >

If you asked me directly after Nicholas was born whether or not I'd have more children, I would've answered with a confident "no way." After the unbearable pain I endured during his birth, I had no idea why anyone would do something like that more than once. The thought of doing all of that again seemed ridiculous. Why have another? So I can be unbelievably nauseous for nine months and then wear a diaper for two more while my boobs throbbed 24/7? No, thank you.

If you asked me six months after Nicholas was born, my answer would have still been "no way," but with a little less of an aggressive tone behind it. I would've said something like, "No way, my son has special needs, and he'll need a lot more attention. I can't allow a new baby to divert that attention when he needs so much extra help. That would just be irresponsible."

Then one day, when Nicholas was about nine months old, I was making dinner in the kitchen while Nicholas played with his toys in the living room. I peeked in to check on him, and he was just sort of sitting and staring at a toy, not doing much. He looked bored and unsure of what to do to entertain himself. I wanted to go in and play with him, but I'd just spent the last hour playing with him and had to get dinner on the table. I thought, *How nice would it be if he had someone to play with?* I always wanted to give my son everything

I could to make him happy. I just never considered that one of those things could be a sibling.

I couldn't tell my husband about my realization right away, because he was already overcome with baby fever. I did the responsible thing and waited to be drunk at a wedding so I could blurt out, "Let's have another baby!"

We became pregnant shortly after that.

When I announced I was pregnant with Marley, I received so many congratulations and well wishes. I also flagged a very common and confusing question.

"Aren't you afraid your next child will have Down syndrome?"

I was so shocked every time I heard it. Obviously, all the advocating I'd been doing for over a year wasn't doing much to sway the thoughts of the people around me in my day-to-day life. They still, deep down, must've thought I had an imperfect child. Even with the happiness we projected as a family, something told them that Nicholas had something wrong with him. They still had yet to see what I saw.

Of course, the thought *had* crossed my mind. I even read from a few sources that your chances of having a baby with Down syndrome go from one in 700 to one in 100 if you already have a child with Down syndrome. But after having Nicholas and learning the truth, I thought it'd be cool to have two children with Down syndrome since it seemed so extremely rare. If anyone were equipped to handle it, it'd be Nick and me. Nicholas would also have someone that he could directly relate to permanently installed in our house, which seemed convenient considering how difficult it can be to find other kids with Down syndrome locally. So, that's what I told everyone when they asked, trying as hard as I could to not be offended by their question. I wanted to make sure that even though the language might make me cringe, people continued to feel they could ask me tough questions about Down syndrome.

That's the only way I can keep the open communication necessary for spreading awareness.

There *was* fear in my mind that had nothing to do with Down syndrome. I'd lived through a surprise chromosomal diagnosis. It nearly killed me. Since then, I've learned about so many other things that could happen before, during, and after birth. I was no longer the blissfully ignorant person I was before Nicholas, and it felt like danger was everywhere. I was so scared to go through the mourning process again. What if I lost the baby? What if the baby had another form of trisomy that wasn't compatible with life? Could I survive the mourning process a second time?

> > >

A little over nine months later, I stared into my husband's hopeful eyes as he waited for me to get up from the diner booth so we could visit our boy one last time. I couldn't seem to formulate any kind of acceptable response. It was like I'd blown a fuse in my brain and needed to be reset. My whole life for the past year and a half had been all about protecting and caring for Nicholas. My free time was consumed with setting up his intervention services and researching Down syndrome topics. I lived and breathed advocacy. Now I was going to be completely distracted with a newborn baby.

What was I thinking?

The braids I asked my friend to put in my hair for the big day suddenly felt suffocatingly tight. It all came rushing back. Childbirth hurts. How could I forget that part? Not to mention it's terrifying. After being through it once already, gruesome scenes from the *Saw* movies don't seem as scary to me anymore. Oh, and the months after? I spent those hidden away in my house riddled with postpartum depression and anxiety. The isolation had been crippling. I couldn't believe I signed up for more torture.

Also, I loved Nicholas more than any other creature on this planet. My love for him was immeasurable. How could I possibly have any love left for this new baby? It couldn't be possible. There was no way I could conjure up any more love than I was already giving to Nicholas.

"I can't" was all I could say out loud. I didn't want Nicholas to make me further lose my nerve. The memories from last time were starting to sting, and I thought if I saw Nicholas, I'd lose it. I'd snatch him up and run away before anyone made me go to the hospital. But I knew the baby would come out one way or the other, so I figured I'd let the professionals help me.

I was in labor for 14 hours with Nicholas, and I pushed for three of them. That's a long time to give one hundred percent of your effort. I was dreading doing that all over again. At around nine p.m. that night, I started pushing for Marley. After my first push, I looked at the clock and thought, *oh crap, another three hours of this is going to suck*. Twenty short minutes later, a fresh baby was put on my chest for some skin-to-skin time. My delicate little angel was here. As I wrapped my arms around her, she popped her head up and looked me right in the eyes.

"Is she okay?" I asked, genuinely worried. It had taken Nicholas months to be able to hold his head up, and weeks to open his eyes that wide. I was startled by her brazen entrance into this world.

"Yes! She's beautiful!" the nurse said as they slurped goop from her throat with an aspirator. Only twenty minutes of pushing followed by an immediate stare-down? I realized then that this was going to be a different experience entirely. I wouldn't know the magnitude of those differences until the next day.

Relieved I was healing so fast and that Marley nursed with ease, I was feeling pretty optimistic. My in-laws brought Nicholas to meet his sister. It was the first time I'd seen him in almost two days, and I missed him like crazy. We let him into the bed with me so he could get a closer look at Marley. He examined her, touched her head, and gave us the best photo opportunities we could've asked for. When Marley started crying, he looked at me as his eyes started to well up, and the visit was cut short. It was the first of many times that her tears caused him to cry too. I was sad to see him leave us, but I was overcome with joy to be holding my new baby girl. My heart *could* love two humans that much, after all. My husband was completely smitten and could barely put her down. The scary part was over. Now, we had two perfect children.

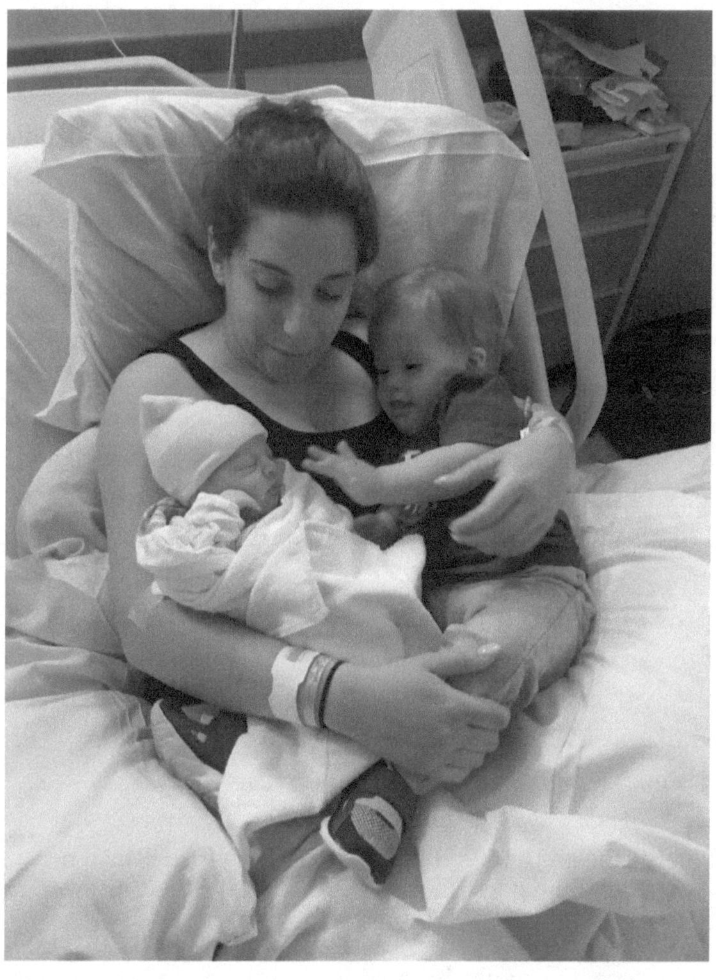

That night Marley started crying, which interrupted my fantasies of our new family of four. She didn't stop for four months. Four long and very loud months. When Marley burst into this world, she came in loud to keep us on our toes. She needed us to know that she is here and that her needs can't be overshadowed by Nicholas's. Message received, Marley.

Those months of having a new baby and a toddler were really difficult, and there were countless times that I didn't feel like I was properly meeting Nicholas's needs. I'll never forget one particular moment when I was left alone with both kids for the first time. Marley needed a diaper change and feeding right away. Nicholas, at that same moment, put his arms up for me to pick him up. To me, when a baby does that, it's the highest honor in the land. I can never turn it down. But in this case, I had to. I was in danger of an incoming diaper mudslide and an inconsolable baby. I said, "I'm so sorry, Nicholas" and walked by him to bring Marley to the changing table.

Nicholas's eyes welled up with tears in response, and so did mine. It was like I'd abandoned him for the newer model, and I could see him feeling that for the first time. This is what I was afraid of all along. I would soon find out that it was all worth it.

The pros outweigh the cons.

All of the anxiety I felt about having more children is now completely overshadowed by the developmental benefits I've seen in Nicholas as a result of Marley's existence. That's right, developmental *benefits*.

Before Marley even came home, I taught Nicholas what "gentle" means so that he didn't give us any close calls when she arrived home. Back then, I would hold newborn Marley in my arms near Nicholas and say "gentle," and he would rub her head oh, so delicately. Now, I can use both siblings to teach in the moment how to be considerate to other people. I can teach them sharing and turn-taking. Or how to not hit your brother on the head with a toy hammer. Marley learned that one eventually, at her own pace, of course. Thanks to Marley, I've been able to teach important lessons in appropriate social interactions without having to rely on his schooling to do that for me.

Siblings help each other grow and develop.

As Marley started making a multitude of new sounds, Nicholas was way more interested in trying them out for himself, and his speech improved as a result. He watched her closely and tried to make the exact sounds she was making, which in turn made her laugh. To them, they were playing a game. These cute exchanges would go on for a long time, and I soaked in every second knowing Nicholas was getting extra practice that he wouldn't have had without her.

The part of Nicholas and Marley's relationship as siblings that interests me most are the interactions they share with no prompting from me. When they play together and communicate using their toddler language, I feel like Jane Goodall trying to decipher the language of the orangutans. I listen to what their little language tries to communicate, and how each of their responses seems to make sense as a reaction. I can't believe that fear of having a sibling for Nicholas almost stopped me from witnessing these awesome moments.

Marley grew to be such a little risk-taker. Once she figured out how to walk, she decided she needed to explore and climb everything in the house. Having Marley around has allowed my super-cautious Nicholas to not only take more risks, but also gain stamina when it comes to using his gross-motor skills. It takes a lot of energy to chase Marley around! I know from experience.

Marley isn't a tough and brave little lady by accident. She was made that way because she's going to have to help Nicholas break some barriers, and she's just the girl for the job.

Now, I don't want you to think that Marley's entire existence was meant as a gift to Nicholas. I've always grown up wanting many children. Not only do I love kids, but I love the idea of a big and close family. Secretly, I've always dreamed of having a little girl. Marley has made my dreams come true in so many ways.

On a day-to-day basis, Nicholas has someone to explore with. When I catch them getting into mischief, I'm happy because I know a lot of communication had to have happened for them to get to that point. One time, I heard the bathroom door shut. When I opened it, Nicholas was in there brushing Marley's hair. He wasn't unraveling all of the toilet paper as I'd expected. He was just loving his sister! His favorite playmate is always in our home and watching them enjoy each other's company is my favorite thing to do.

Marley being born diagnosis-free has redefined me as a mother. When it was just Nicholas, I saw myself as a "special needs mom" only, especially considering all of the advocating I'd had to do at that point in my journey. Now, I'm just a mom, and having the opportunity to advocate for my kids is just a small part of what that means.

Lesson 18

Never stop advocating.

Opportunities to advocate always pop up when I least expect it. When I was new to this, I wouldn't know how to react to people's comments. I had no plan for what I'd say if someone said something questionable about my son. Would I correct them? Would I ignore it? Of course, confrontations are uncomfortable, but they're even more so when you don't feel prepared for them.

Before Nicholas, I didn't truly understand the nature of advocating. To me, it was something more deliberate and planned. Maybe an awareness walk or shared social media post could've been seen to me as advocating. Now I know being a true advocate is something much different. It weaves its way into every aspect of my life, whether I planned it or not. It's something I have to be prepared to do at all times because I'll never know when I need to use my advocacy tools.

What is an advocate? An advocate could be anyone with or without a disability or membership in a minority group who goes out of their way to speak out or stick up for someone else. In my case, I spread awareness about Down syndrome to advocate for my son so more people know the real deal about Down syndrome. But I also advocate for him by making sure that his IEP is being followed or that he's getting the same opportunities as his typical peers. There are endless ways I can advocate for my son. Since I began, I learned it's something that I'd better get good at because it's a never-ending job.

Other people can benefit from your advocating efforts. The typically developing kids of the world can get just as much value from advocacy as children with Down syndrome can. It's important to teach kids to be accepting of all people and to know how to interact with all people. If my students had never heard of Down syndrome, they might be scared or nervous when they meet someone with Down syndrome. On the flip side, if they know all about it, they'll know they can treat that person the same as anyone else. Perhaps one of them will grow up to have a child with Down syndrome, and thanks to their experience in my classroom, they won't be afraid.

> > >

One day, while sitting in our "family circle," I asked my students why they thought I was a teacher. I like to start each day with some thought-provoking questions to get their minds warmed up, and we were having a conversation about why people do what they do. At the time, there were famous people spreading messages of ignorance and hate in the media, and I had a feeling my students were privy to it. In an attempt to steer the conversation in that direction, we talked about why they were in school. I followed up by asking them why I was.

A lot of hands shot up. "Money."

This made me chuckle. Teachers are famously not in it for the riches.

"Yeah, yeah, yeah, forget the money. Sure, I need money to live and pay for things like food and shelter, but what else? What am I doing here? What good does this do for *me*? Why don't I work somewhere else and get money some other way?"

The kids thought long and hard about this.

One boy shyly raised his hand. "Hugs?"

Giggles rippled through our circle while some cheeks flushed.

"Oh, yes. That is a major perk of my job here. Unlimited hugs from friends. What else?"

The kids looked at one another as they thought about it. Another student raised his hand. "Friends?"

"Definitely," I said. "That's another great advantage of being a teacher. I get to have all of you as my best friends! What else?" At this point, they seemed to be out of ideas. Money, hugs, friends—all of the most important things to them were already spoken for.

It's an interesting thing, but I usually get the most meaningful and thoughtful responses in conversations with my class from the students who'd never openly volunteer themselves during an academic lesson. This was one of those times.

"You can teach us that Down syndrome is cool."

Immediately, a huge smile took over my face. I wasn't even going to take the conversation there. Well, I sort of was, but not specifically geared toward Down syndrome. This kid picked right upon it, and if you hadn't already guessed, it was the same boy who asked me if he had Down syndrome a month or so earlier.

"And why would I want to do that?"

The student explained that if I teach them that Down syndrome is cool then they'll be nice to people they meet with Down syndrome instead of bully them or be confused by them. We'd already established earlier in the year that they were more like people with Down syndrome than they were different, so why not treat those people as they deserve to be treated? Isn't that what we want ourselves? And what about all those other differences? Should we hate them and fear them just because we don't know about them? Many of the students didn't even know about Down syndrome before my lesson on the subject.

I told them that sometimes, people who have a lot of people listening to them use that opportunity to spread sadness or hate toward people they don't quite understand yet. Those people who listen to them trust their opinion and might agree with them strictly because they're famous. I explained that I wanted to be a teacher to spread good messages to all the people who listen to me. These good messages include the acceptance of diverse people all over the world. The things the students said during this family circle were so amazing. They gave me so many other examples of meaningful messages I should teach to all my future students so they'll be good and kind people. I wish I could see the world as they see it.

"We have to listen to you every day. It's what school is all about. So, you should probably tell us nice things instead of mean things. It's like, why would we want to sit here and learn mean things?"

There's nothing like the pure honesty and wisdom of a kid.

Of course, when this particular family meeting took place, I was a little more seasoned in talking about Down syndrome. As you know, that wasn't always the case.

In my first month back at work, a student saw a picture of my son and said, "Aw! He's so cute. He doesn't even look like he has Down syndrome!"

Even though this student meant to compliment Nicholas and his immeasurable cuteness, I couldn't help but wonder if she considered traits of Down syndrome to be flawed, so to her, not looking like he has Down syndrome makes him cute. I used that as a teachable moment and pointed out all of the physical markers of Down syndrome to her, gushing over how each one was just so adorable. I wanted to show her that he wasn't cute *despite* his diagnosis. He was just born a cutie! Others that year would act shocked if I reported some sort of developmental milestone as if they couldn't believe he was already finding success in those areas. These opportunities inform the language and ideas that people have about Down syndrome come up so frequently it surprises me every time. Whenever it happens, I can't help but think about the times that Nicholas will deal with these situations without me.

Raise your kids to advocate for themselves.

Even though he's still so young, I worry about Nicholas being equipped to advocate for himself once he enters public school. As a member of that universe, I sometimes see people help children with disabilities more than they need. Maybe they feel bad for them. Maybe they want them to move faster out of frustration. Maybe, worst of all, they truly believe the child to be incapable of performing the tasks they are asking of them.

Over-helping a child can hinder development and attribute to learned helplessness. If Nicholas has someone feed him his lunch with a spoon every day, he'll never learn to feed himself with a spoon efficiently. If someone always helps him put his backpack on, he'll never learn how to do it himself. A child can become complacent in situations like this and assume there will always be an adult around to get them their pencil or tie their shoelaces without them having to ask on their own.

This is not what I want for Nicholas. I've already had to combat stereotypes countless times during his life, and he needs to learn how to do the same. I don't want people to assume he can't do things just because he has Down syndrome. I'm sure that when Nicholas is older, he'll feel the same. No one wants to be underestimated. I can barely stand when it happens to me. If Nicholas wants to do things in life like get a job or go to college, I want him to feel confident enough in his independence to be able to do so.

For these reasons, I'm teaching Nicholas to advocate for his independence. This way, if he's in a situation where he's getting more help than he needs, he can say, "No, thank you, I can do it myself." There's more to it than making sure he's independent. If people who aren't associated with Nicholas see him having everything done for him, then they'll think he *needs* everything done for him. Although we don't want to worry too much about what other people think, it's important to change the perception of the general public about Down syndrome whenever we have the opportunity.

Through my experience, I've constantly found myself debunking common misconceptions surrounding Down syndrome. I've proven my own beliefs wrong, in a good way. Sometimes, the opportunities to advocate are planned. Other times, they spring up out of the blue. Either way, I've found that when it comes to advocating, actions speak way louder than words.

Lesson 19

Show, don't tell.

When I was worried about my son's new diagnosis, statistics didn't help. When I was worried about his development, articles didn't help. When I was worried about his health, the research didn't help. I couldn't just read facts.

I needed to *see* what real life was going to be like.

The thing that saved me from my lowest point was the ability to observe other families living their awesome lives on social media. I can't imagine where I'd be if I'd never been exposed to other families who had children with Down syndrome. There's no way I'd be the advocate I am today. For us to build these life-saving communities that exist on the internet, someone needs to be willing to be open up first. If they hadn't, I'd be nowhere near where I am today on my path of healing and resilience. Over the years, I've had the best time paying it forward. When I do, I try to keep in mind that showing Nicholas's successes says a lot more about Down syndrome than constantly spewing facts to the world.

Sharing your life with the world can bring unexpected blessings.

One day in early 2019 while perusing social media during my morning scroll time, I was looking at some amazing families who had children with Down syndrome. I follow a lot of them, as well as a lot of organizations that are meant to spread awareness. My newsfeed is always filled with adorable and inspiring faces. I noticed an organization called Nothing Down I'd followed since the beginning of my journey had put out an ad looking for new ambassadors. These ambassadors would use the Nothing Down platform to showcase their lives so that the public could see there was "nothing down" about Down syndrome.

I'd seen the same advertisement the previous year and knew that hundreds of people applied. I watched as some kids were chosen and followed their stories as they worked to spread awareness in their communities. They did fundraisers, walks, school tours, and news interviews. Since the first part of the application was a quick form, I thought, *What do I have to lose? This'll only take a minute.* I applied, then forgot all about it.

A week or so later, I received an email from Nothing Down requesting more information about our family's story. I sent in the requested information, trying not to get too excited. I wondered what it would be like for Nicholas to be an ambassador for this organization. Would it be much different than what we were doing with our current online presence? I accidentally got my hopes up, which is something I rarely allow myself to do. I'm known to protect myself from disappointment at all costs. I shared this application with my family and got their hopes up too. Luckily, I didn't have to be so cautious, because a while later, I got an email saying that Nicholas had been selected to be a global ambassador for Nothing Down!

This was a transformational moment for me. It was the moment I went from being the crying mother feeling sorry for herself in the rocking chair while looking at Instagram to being the mom who was on the screen, showing the world there was nothing to feel sorry about. I was the family in the sandcastle picture. I made the transition from the receiver of hope to the giver. We could now become a family that helped someone who's still grieving the life they had by showing them that the best was yet to come. Maybe there's a new mother out there sitting in her rocking chair with her newborn looking at us right now.

At the very beginning of his ambassadorship, I was interviewed by the local newspaper. When I was done with the interview, the journalist told me it'd be in the paper the next morning. I was pretty excited, but with the hustle and bustle of another school day, I almost forgot to pull into the gas station by my house to check the newspaper racks on my way to work. I went in to check the paper, thinking I'd have to flip through for a minute to find it. Instead, I was shocked to see his adorable face plastered right on the front page with the headline "Minetto Toddler Selected as Global Ambassador for Nothing Down." I grabbed a small stack of them and giddily brought them to the register, telling everyone I saw on the way "that's my son!" The strangers at the gas station were not all that impressed, but my classroom family sure was. I could always count on them to share in my joy. "Mrs. Goewey, Nicholas is famous!"

Nicholas became more of a local celebrity than he already was. He appeared on multiple news channels, he was on the front page of a few newspaper publications, and I was frequently being asked to be a guest blogger for various advocacy websites. Through these multiple channels, I didn't have to stand on a soapbox and shout his worth to the world. People were able to see it from their usual news outlets. It allowed us to spread awareness and acceptance on a global scale, and not just to people who looked for it such as the people I suspect already read my blog. We even had a camera crew at the house to film a show that aired on PBS where we were able to squash some common misconceptions about Down syndrome. None of this would've been possible without the platform given to us by Nothing Down.

Be prepared for the occasional unsupportive comment. Sadly, there are people on the internet who don't wish to see their misconceptions proven wrong. I wasn't ready for some of the comments people left on the blog and Instagram attempting to spread hateful messages. This was a hard concept for me to grasp because even though I know cyberbullying exists, I never expected to see grown adults attacking a small child for having a developmental disability. They'd comment asking me to stop posting lies and would use the r-word when referring to my son, who was only two years old. They would also give me some made-up statistics hoping to prove to me that he wouldn't amount to anything. For some reason, though, the mean comments didn't upset me as much as I thought they would. Instead, they fueled my fire, giving me new topics to write about in my blog. Those who follow my blog and don't have a child with Down syndrome are just as surprised about these internet "trolls" as I was. The parents who have a child with Down syndrome usually aren't, because they get messages like that too.

Some meme pages on the internet post memes making fun of people with Down syndrome. For example, I saw one where a popular children's cartoon character was made to look like it had the physical features of Down syndrome so that it could park in a handicapped parking space. The actual meme didn't hurt me. The thought of Nicholas seeing it when he's old enough to understand was the painful part. For that reason, I feel even more inclined to show the world what Down syndrome is really like so people like the person who created that meme become fewer in numbers, and hopefully much more compassionate.

I always try to immediately turn to empathy instead of anger when I see comments or memes like that because I have something these people don't have. I have the privilege of knowing people with Down syndrome. I usually either use the comments as a teachable moment or delete them altogether.

The only thing that bothers me about it is that someday, Nicholas will know how to read and be able to see these things. It's impossible for me to spread enough awareness to silence the ignorance by then, and the scale of that job is overwhelming. I almost left these hurtful things out of this book because I didn't want to scare new parents by telling them about the hate we've encountered. However, I think it's important to note that there are people out there who are set in their beliefs when it comes to special needs. These will be the toughest nuts to crack, and we have to work together to change their perceptions.

> > >

For World Down Syndrome Day 2020, we had a plan to do a classroom tour around our school district and give students the opportunity that I didn't have growing up, which was the chance to interact directly with someone with Down syndrome. Sadly, just a week or so earlier, everything closed down due to the COVID-19 pandemic. It's a good thing we live in a time where social media can reach plenty of people regardless of distance.

A show on PBS caught wind of Nicholas's ambassadorship and asked us to be a part of their documentary series called *Cycle of Health*. A camera crew came to our house and interviewed us while getting footage of the kids playing together. When the show finally aired, my husband and I were both in tears. We couldn't believe that in the span of a little over two years, we'd gotten to the point where we were talking about this on public television. We went from never speaking of it to invading people's living rooms with our story.

Seeing people with Down syndrome doing amazing things in the world gives me so much hope and excitement for Nicholas. In the hospital, I was so limited in what I thought he could accomplish in his life. I wondered about all of the things he wouldn't be able to do, which is crazy because in three short years he's reached the world on a global scale. Now, I look at him and see his unlimited potential. He has caused Nick and me to follow dreams we didn't know we had. He's brought joy to so many people. I look forward to the work we can do as he gets older and hopefully, wants to become more involved. To have my best buddy as my teammate in this journey will only make it more fun.

Lesson 20

Our future is limitless.

I started this journey with flaws I hadn't even acknowledged. I lived in a reality where I was able to control all aspects of my life. When Nicholas was born, I thought I'd never have control of my life again. I assumed there was no way I could reach the dreams I had. I thought I'd have to spend my life trying to convince Nicholas he could do anything. Without trying, he was able to give that gift to me instead. As I reflect back on how afraid I was of Nicholas's diagnosis changing our lives, I really had no idea how amazing those changes would be.

We thought life as we knew it was over, and we were right. Without even trying, Nicholas has given us futures that are far superior to the ones we'd laid out for ourselves.

When he was born, my husband was running a restaurant in town. His shift was two p.m. until whenever the restaurant closed that night. He'd often home in the wee hours of the morning only to get up at seven a.m. with Nicholas and start the day all over again. It was a good schedule for us when he was a baby and we didn't want to send him to a babysitter right away, but as he started getting older, Nick realized he was in danger of missing some big moments in Nicholas's life. How could he ever attend a basketball game or a school concert if he was always working in the evenings? I certainly didn't want to do all of those things alone, either. I wanted Nicholas to grow up with both of his parents in his corner, and so did my husband.

Because of this, we decided to have Nick quit his job at the restaurant to become a barber's apprentice. That meant he'd go from making a good salary to no salary at all. He went from being the boss to being the lowest-ranking member of the staff, all to spend more time with our son. He didn't do it because Nicholas needed more support than a typical child; he did it because Nicholas had wholly won him over, and he didn't want to miss a minute of his adventure.

This change depleted all the money we had saved up, and we signed up to struggle financially for a while, but the idea of missing out on our family being whole for Nicholas was even scarier. Nicholas gave Nick the future he wanted, one as a dad who's both involved and available. Now, Nick works at a job he loves, surrounded by guys he considers close friends and doing something that satisfies the artist in him, all while being able to be with his family the moment we might need him.

Nicholas gave that same gift to me. I'm a teacher, but I originally went to college for creative writing. It's always been my dream to write and publish books. However, once I fell into the comfortable routine of my teaching career, I forgot all about that. It didn't feel like I needed to pursue that dream anymore since I truly love my career.

Since I've broadened my thinking to envision Nicholas doing all any amazing things he'll ever want to do, I extended that way of thinking to myself. Instead of thinking, *I can't be a writer because I'm a teacher*, I started thinking, *It's a good thing I'm a teacher because I can write my books during the summer months.* Now, I'm writing and publishing books on my own. I would've never had the confidence in myself to do that if it weren't for the confidence Nicholas has inspired inside me. I'm fulfilling concrete dreams I used to have because of his existence in my life.

It's okay to still be afraid sometimes.

I'd be lying if I painted myself as this fearless special needs mom who's ready for anything that comes her way. Although Nicholas's having Down syndrome no longer scares me, I still have fear. I'm afraid of Nicholas not being invited to birthday parties or playdates. I'm afraid that other kids won't be able to easily connect with him because his speech isn't as developed as theirs. I'm afraid that he might think of himself as an outcast if there isn't a local community of other kids with Down syndrome. I'd hate for him to experience the isolation that I felt in the beginning. What do all of these fears have in common? I have zero control over any of them.

The fear mindset is easy to slip into when you have a child with Down syndrome. All we want is what every other parent wants: for their child to be happy and feel accepted by others. All I can do is make sure Nicholas is well-prepared for what life may bring his way and try to build up his confidence so that he's comfortable in his skin. It's okay to be afraid, and as long as I can recognize it, I can focus on the ways that I can help.

This entire experience has changed how I react to life events in general. Things I would've seen as a crisis before don't have nearly the same impact on me now. Marley, at about a year old, started doing this thing where she would tense up for seemingly no reason, although I'm sure she had one. She'd be playing with the dog or sitting in her highchair and making two fists, tensing her whole body up for a second. Once in a while, it would be followed by a little grunt. I know what you're thinking, and no, she wasn't pooping.

Before Nicholas I would've panicked about this, immediately thinking there was something "wrong" with my daughter. Instead, one day after witnessing one of the many instances, I thought, *It's so weird I'm not concerned about that one bit.* I really didn't care to investigate it at the time because for all I knew, she was just alleviating a stimulatory sensation she was craving. It wasn't hurting her or anyone else and didn't seem like an immediate threat.

The old me would have researched myself into an early grave about something that would probably go away with time. I'm so thankful to this experience for giving me a more relaxed and patient approach to parenting. My friends who have kids are always telling me they wish they were as relaxed as me when it comes to parenting, but after going through this experience, I just can't sweat the small stuff.

Instead, I use all of the energy I would've used to stress out to celebrate all of life's little successes. Nicholas knows I'm watching his development closely, not because he knows he has Down syndrome, but because he loves celebrating his accomplishments with me. He always wants to show me what he can do, and it fills my heart with joy every single time.

Nicholas has also taught me it's okay if my way of thinking is more fluid than concrete. The identity crisis I had as a result of the diagnosis happened because I wasn't used to challenging my ways of thinking. It completely rocked my mental boat, and I had no clue how to steer forward. I know now that it's okay not to know everything and questioning what you think you know is a completely acceptable practice.

Don't fear the future, look forward to it.

The experience I went through as a result of Nicholas's diagnosis surely wasn't a happy one at first. There were days where I felt like I could crawl into a hole and die. All of those emotions were a result of my underlying fear for the future. I was scared of a future I'd never had the chance to picture. I was afraid our lives were over. As tumultuous as it was, I wouldn't trade a single second. The wide range of emotions I was able to tap into has made me who I am today. My perspective has evolved and I'm more equipped to show empathy to others than I ever was. Those deep dark moments showed me the true value that a community of people with shared experiences. If I just continued thinking that my experiences alienated me from society, I would probably still be held up in my house riddled with fear. Thankfully, through community, I learned the future is nothing to be afraid of.

Reflecting on that fact makes me think about the mothers of children with Down syndrome in history. I've become intrigued by the impact that community can have on the repercussions of trauma and was interested to see if mothers of the past were able to find one of their own. Without technology, they would've never been able to stumble upon families that looked just like theirs. They would then have no way to reach out to those families who could've helped normalize their feelings. As I attempted to research mothers speaking out about their child's Down syndrome diagnosis, I found nothing more than internet databases that perpetuated stereotypes. Sadly, those search results weren't that old. Parents who read those things first must be overwhelmed with fear, which makes it hard to look forward to the future.

So many good things have happened to me simply because Nicholas exists. That has been the one constant through this experience, and I can't help but look forward to whatever the future holds for us, even with all the unknowns.

Many mothers both in the past and present have been told their child would never and could never amount to anything. To hear those words from a source you're supposed to trust is heartbreaking. Instead of trusting someone who likely doesn't have a child with Down syndrome, trust the stories of other mothers. I've walked this path already, and my son has amounted to so much in only three short years. I'm so grateful every day that I don't have to feel shame when it comes to shouting my son's worth to the world. As he gets older, I won't have to do much shouting. Nicholas can win over the masses by merely existing, growing, learning, and proving that he can do anything. He's taught me more in his three years of existence than I can ever hope to teach him.

Most importantly, Nicholas has shown me our future is not limited because of Down syndrome. My little boy got famous not because people feel bad for him, but because he inspires them. Watching how hard he works at such a young age to be successful inspires me to work harder every day. He does everything with a passion that I wish I could replicate. The thought of the future fills me with immeasurable excitement, leaving very little room for fear. Thanks to Nicholas, I can finally see our family has a truly limitless life.

Acknowledgements

There have been so many people in my life who have helped me make this book a reality. I could never dream of doing them justice in such a small passage, but I'm sure going to try.

First, I'd like to thank Amy Shore for inviting me into her home just to plant the seed in my mind that I should write a book. You saw this book before I did, and your belief in me is the reason that it finally exists.

To my Limitless Nicholas community, you have brought so much joy to my life. Your support has meant so much to our family. Thank you for helping me share Nicholas's story across the globe and for encouraging me to keep sharing every single day.

Annie Urckfitz, my friend and fellow writer. Thank you for helping me build this book through an endless stream of voice memos. You gave me the confidence to make this book as raw and honest as I could.

Alison Meaker, my dear friend and colleague. Whenever it seemed like I'd taken on too much while writing this book, you were there to tell me I was going to crush it. Thank you from the bottom of my heart.

To my fellow Down syndrome parents, you are the tribe I never knew I needed. Thank you for knowing exactly what I need to hear and for helping me be a stronger mother every single day.

To the friends in our circle, thank you for loving Nicholas and raising your children to love him just as he is. You accepted him immediately and made sure that we never felt alone. I adore the family we have built together.

Dean and Linda, my mother- and father-in-law. This book wouldn't exist without your support, encouragement, and willingness to babysit my wacky children whenever a deadline approached. You both mean the world to me.

Thank you, Mom, for raising me to believe I can do anything and for always supporting me while I attempt to bring those dreams to life. Dad, thank you for making me outgoing enough to make my life so public. Tony, thank you for always being my cheerleader and supporting my creative endeavors. You three are the foundation on which I stand.

Nick, my husband and best friend. This book, along with every other good thing in my life, wouldn't be a reality without you. Thank you for pushing me to finish this massive project even when it got in the way of our lives from time to time. I love the life we've built together. I love you endlessly.

Finally, to my loves Nicholas and Marley. You two are my heart and soul. You make me want to accomplish everything I've ever dreamed of, but being your mom is my greatest accomplishment of all. You two are my life's greatest joy.

Resources and References

My belief will always be that the best resources for parents of children with Down syndrome are and will always be fellow parents. Below is the list of resources that I mention in this book along with some amazing websites that have brought me hope throughout my journey.

National Down Syndrome Society (ndss.org)
This advocacy group provides the world with up-to-date policy changes, statistics, and community outreach programs. Their website has amazing resources for people with Down syndrome and their families.

Nothing Down (nothingdown.org)
This organization is near and dear to my heart. They create videos and other content that help educate people about Down syndrome. They present their content to schools, medical professionals, and anyone else who may have a stake in a child's life. Started by two moms with a dream, they have spread awareness across the globe.

I Thought It Was Just Me (But It Isn't) by Brené Brown
This is the book that I referenced in the introduction. It taught me that I'm not alone in my journey, and never will be.

My favorite families to follow on social media:
@nothingdownaboutit
@downwithjaxandniko
@perfectlypierce
@thehouseofwheeler

About the Author

Mary Goewey is a blogger, author, and educator based in New York. Her works are geared toward supporting and including differently-abled people and their families.

To keep up with her family and upcoming projects, follow her on social media.

Instagram:
@mary_goewey
@limitlessnicholas

Websites:
www.marygoewey.com
www.limitlessnicholas.com

www.ingramcontent.com/pod-product-compliance
Lightning Source LLC
LaVergne TN
LVHW091140080826
845145LV00008B/2215

* 9 7 8 1 7 3 7 6 1 4 4 0 1 *